My Life in War
Did We Ever Really Leave

By Joshua Apel

To my lovely wife and beautiful daughter, Hannah, and to every man and woman who has risked their lives and given their lives to the service of their country....this book is yours.

To the readers: I am not a professional writer by any means. The content of this book was printed only so that I can tell the world my story so more people can hopefully understand what it was like for me while I was deployed in support of Operation Iraqi Freedom.

-Me

PRELUDE

Albert Camus once said, "In such a world of conflict, a world of victims and executioners, it is the job of thinking people, not to be on the side of executioners". His philosophies included the thought that we value our lives but know that we will eventually die. I think he was on to something there, clearly he knew that with life come death and no matter how much we try or how hard we fight. Someday we die. It's just a matter of what you do in between that makes life so important. For a soldier, these are words to live by. We all come from different worlds, different backgrounds, rich families and broken homes. We are raised in different environments by completely different people and yet in some way, somehow, something brings us all together to the same world to accomplish the same goal. We may have different opinions of our goal; to serve our country, to protect our families from terrorists, to defend The United States Constitution. We are brought to this earth together to fight and possibly die to protect the life of the man to our left and our right. To risk everything we have in our lives to ensure that our brothers get home to their families. And if we should fall at the hand of our enemy, we did it for a reason and that is what makes us different from the rest of the world. A friend asked me once, "Josh, why do you fight for a country filled with people that hate you?" The answer is simple; the next time you are in an airport and you see a soldier returning home from combat and you see a little boy or girl run straight up to him and jump into his arms, take a look. thats why.

CHAPTER 1

I can still smell the smoke; the stale black thickness that filled my nostrils and burned my lungs as we maneuvered our Strykers through the crowds of thousands. They were there to protest us and they would fight to the death if it meant taking at least one of our lives. I stand strong in my hatch overlooking the people, commanding my driver to slowly push through them, careful to not hit any of them. I look left and scan the roof tops and windows of a broken old building and slowly scan right back over the crowd and suddenly a loud bang

Darkness: I see nothing or hear nothing but my own heartbeat as I rise up from my back covered in sweat. My eyesight slowly returns and I began to check myself for injuries only to realize that right next to me I see a beautiful red haired woman fast asleep with her back to me. I lean over and kiss her head and drag my feet from under the blanket setting them on the cold floor. I take a deep breath to recover from last night's dream. The same dream I have had many times before, and wake up to the same beautiful sight, has haunted me for over a year now. The distant memory of a time in my life that I can never get back and can never forget the daily horrors of screaming women and children, ear piercing explosions, and the unending sound of enemy bullets flying past your face.

I am an American Soldier in the United States Army. I have served for over years now, and have spent more than two years of that time in a combat zone. I was part of a different sort of unit, then. We were the first Brigade to take a new vehicle called, The Stryker, to combat. The Stryker is a 2ton, 8 wheeled Infantry Carrier Vehicle and for the majority of our time there, this vehicle would be our home, our armor, our fire power and sometimes even our bed.

In my first deployment I spent most of the time as a Rifle Squad Team Leader, but the last deployment I was the Vehicle Commander for my Company Commanders Stryker. We were out nearly every time another platoon was out and whenever there was a fight we were right there laying the smack down on the enemy.

Now, over a year later, I am an Instructor at the Stryker Bradley Instructional Company with the Stryker Master Trainer Team. In a nutshell, I teach others how to do what I did while I was deployed and to give them the information and tools that they need to go back to their Units and teach other soldiers the same. Although I don't get to fire my weapon in anger any more,

or I don't face the dangers of being blown up, I can still shut my eyes and remember what it was like in my first fire fight.
I can still remember what it felt like the first time I ever heard an IED (Improvised Explosive Device) blow up nearby.

Although, I come home every day after work to my wife as if I was part of a normal life, with a brief case and a cup of coffee, I still feel like a part of me never came home. I catch myself trying to remember certain things about my experience and the brothers that I met there and ask myself if I was ever really there, did I ever really leave. And now my wonderful wife, Mindy, who constantly reminds me of how lucky I am to be alive, has helped me recover from my wounds and memories. She has stuck around through many nights of jumping out of bed ready to fight, excessive drinking, constant arguing, and sometimes unbelievable depression and anxiety.

Products of war, these symptoms have become my new combat zone in a sense and, although, I have gotten over most of them there will always be a hint of them sneaking up behind me at any moment.
What I am about to share with you, you may never understand. Some of you, probably combat veterans yourselves, may have been through similar and even worst experiences. I know that my war is different from everyone else's and their experiences are their own. But these are my experiences and thoughts of a time when I was this man.

CHAPTER 2
Back for round 2

3June 2006, we have already landed in Kuwait, and already I am tired. Almost a full day of nothing but traveling from Fort Lewis, Washington to here and I can already feel the tension around me. I think about the things that I left back in the states but it already seems like a distant memory, clouded by the emotions and anxiety of what was to come of us for the next year or so.

Myself, SGT Joshua Apel, and my brothers here with me are part of an Infantry Unit unlike the rest of the Army has ever seen. We are still Grunts and we still train to fight just like any other Infantry soldier out there, but we are different. We have something that only a limited part of the Army has; Strykers. We have all the same fire-power and we can still deliver unimaginable force to the enemy when needed but we have the ability to get onto the objective, get the enemy, and be off the objective before anyone knows we were there.

The Stryker is a 20-ton, 8 wheeled Infantry Carrier. It has a 35horsepower engine and can give the enemy a run for their money in a firefight. But, that is not what makes the Stryker so lethal. Combined with a M2 .50caliber machine gun, or a MK-19 Grenade Machine Gun, and enough armor to protect us against a lot of crap this vehicle stops on the objective and out of the back of the vehicle comes one of the Army's most highly trained and lethal Infantryman. They exit the ramp in broad daylight or in the stealth of night armed and trained for anything the enemy has waiting. And they are damn good at it.

This isn't the first time most of us have been here, though there are a lot of fresh faces. Over a year and a half ago we were here preparing to drive North across the Iraq border as the first Stryker Brigade ever to see combat. We were ready last time and we are ready this time. But, if there is one thing our training has taught us it's this; nothing ever goes to plan!

This time, we have taken a couple stops on the way here, first in Maine where we were met with a lot of supporters who had plenty of hand-shakes and hugs to give us before we left the states and then to Germany where we had a chance to make a few phone calls and tell our families and loved-ones that we were ok. Now we are in Camp Udari, Kuwait where I have finally gotten a chance to sit and take all this in again.

This is the same Camp where we arrived in 2003 for our Baptism by Fire as the press and our old Commanders would say. I remember the familiar, dry heat and sand quickly blowing into my eyes and mouth just as quickly as I could shut them. We have been put into large tents that fit a lot of our Company. And almost as quickly as I get my cot and sit down, we are called to help carry in all the heavy weapons and equipment to a make-shift arms room.

Our Company, Charlie Company of the 1st and 23rd Infantry Division, is a quite unique group of soldiers young and old. Almost immediately, as we work, the Team Leaders and Squad Leaders start grabbing up the newer soldiers to help carry in the gear and every once in a while stop a couple of them so that they may perform their best version of I'm a Little Teapot. They can see that these Cherries are a little nervous and completely unaware of what may happen and they call them out to lighten the mood and assure them that even though we are in this mess, we can still have a little fun. The soldiers perform with perfection and a bright smile on their face, knowing that their leaders and the experienced members of their squads have been through exactly what they are going through.

We are supposed to be here, In Kuwait, for a short period of time before heading across the border and arrive, eventually, to FOB (Forward Operating Base) Summerall. I know what can and probably will happen on the way there, but I can hardly wait for some reason. I don't even think about anything back in the states at this point because we are here now. Anything back home is pointless if I don't start thinking about the objective at hand. I know I have to start focusing on our mission because my life and the life of my brothers next to me depend on it.

The work was finally finished and at the entrance of our tent is a clutter of weapon cages and large wooden boxes. We have all the equipment we need except for one important thing; Strykers. They are still on the boat headed to the port where a lot of us will head to and pick them up before prepping them for transport across the border and until they arrive our days will be nothing but training and getting acclimatized to the grueling heat that surrounds us.

For now all we can do is lie down for the night and try to get some sleep, but I know in the back of my mind that a lot of us will get little sleep tonight. We are tired, but wide awake at the same time trying to mentally prepare for anything that can come at us once we move into Iraq. We run through scenario after scenario of everything that we have been training for hoping that it was enough to prepare us. I can feel my eyes get heavy as my thoughts begin to turn into dreams and I slowly drift to sleep, surrounded by a completely different world as far away from home as we can get.

1 July 2006, I woke up today ready to kick the day off with the first breakfast in country. I am dressed in my PT (Physical Training) uniform as I head out the door of our tent into the already blistering heat of Kuwait. Just as it was last deployment, we have been put in tents as far away from the chow hall as they could put us. We don't know why they did this again, but we write it off as politics thinking that we are Grunts and don't deserve to be put near the rest of the POGs (People Other than Grunts) on this Camp. I guess they are afraid we will destroy their precious Camp or will cause a scene, but for whatever reason we are here and we immediately start looking for alternate modes of transportation to get us to the Chow Hall for some much needed food.

Today, we get some down time as our bodies begin to adjust to the new climate. In Washington the year is full of about months of rain and usually cloudy. There is a couple months of the year where we can enjoy the outdoors by heading to the lake or just getting out and enjoying the night life of Tacoma or Seattle, however the temperature usually sticks around 7 to 8 degrees in the Summer time. At 0500 hours in the morning, here in Kuwait, it is already 113 degrees and there is no breeze at all. I put my sunglasses on and look left towards the direction of the chow hall and can make out the roof of it from where I am standing.

I take in a deep breath before I sling my weapon to my back and take in a whiff of the Port-O-Toilets not even 5feet from our tents. The only thing I can tell you about the crappers is that it's the only place to get any sort of privacy and you can lose a lot of water weight in just a few minutes of being in them. The sauna-like temperature inside them feels nearly double of what it is outside and walking out of them is almost like stepping into an air conditioned room for a couple minutes. I shake the stench and head for the Chow Hall.

My first breakfast, and I will never forget it, was biscuits and gravy, sausage, breakfast burritos, an apple fritter, and some juice. I love breakfast and quickly take advantage of the good chow that they have here in Camp Udari. It's no wonder this place is full of soldiers who spend almost an entire deployment here. These are the soldiers that go home after a deployment full of war stories and a big fat combat patch on their right shoulders. We call them FOBBITS for they make the FOB their homes for the entire tour. They eat up all the food, take up all the space in the MWR tents and buy everything from the PX that they can. But as useless as they may sound, we still need them. Without Support Units the Infantry would be without a lot of much needed amenities such as chow, mail, fresh water, supplies and much more.

I return from my meal a little bit fatter, and ready to lie back down on my cot and watch a movie on my portable DVD player. Among all the gear we pack, we have prepared ourselves for this deployment by bringing with us portable DVD players and MP3 players although the only thing we need as much as we need water is a deck of playing cards. Strung out all over the tent our Company has broken into small groups playing games like Poker, Black Jack, Spades and even Solitaire. Some of them even have poker chips and immediately begin a game of Texas Hold Em that carries on throughout the rest of the deployment as much a tradition as chow time.

In my tent are our entire Headquarters Platoon and 3rd Platoon. We aren't rivals but there is always a lot of trash talk between us and even though most of it is directed toward my platoon, Headquarters, I don't get upset because even though some of my HQ brothers may never leave the wire on a mission I am my Company Commanders VC (Vehicle Commander) and will spend much of my time off the FOB whenever a platoon leaves for a raid or patrol. So along with their smack talk I have much of my own to give them back.

I was with 3rd Platoon last time we were here and have sense become a VC. Our First Sergeant always says that in order to become a good Squad Leader in a Stryker Platoon, its best to have experience as a VC so that was my intention when I became one. However, since I started as a VC I have loved it. There is a great feeling in knowing that if our boys got on and off the objective it was because I got them there. If a platoon was pinned down in a fire fight I could easily get close to the enemy and lay down hell on them with my machine gun. I got more trigger time as a VC than I ever did as a squad member and that was enough to keep me in the Gunners seat. Besides the fact that I was the only VC in the Company that my Commander trusted and refused to let me go but I didn't argue.

The guys from 3rd Platoon and I have always been close. I spent my first few years with Charlie Company in that Platoon. I have partied with them, gotten in trouble with them, started fights with them, and their leadership has made me the soldier I am today. They are rowdy as hell and will stop at nothing to get the job done. I look around with my headphones on and watch them constantly punching each other, scuffing up their Joes, throwing stuff around the tent and passing around computers with endless amounts of porn, another amenity needed by most grunts in a place like this.

I look up at the ceiling listening to my headphones and start to drift into a nap until about mid after noon; the power went out in the tent. I woke up in a pool of sweat and most of the tent had already escaped to the outside crouching into what little shade the large tent provided. We sat outside for a couple of hours, but it seemed like forever when the power finally came back on. Whoever was hired to keep the generators running wasn't doing their job and it ran out of fuel. Most likely the Army had hired local contractors to perform these sorts of duties and more such as pumping the crappers and other odd jobs around the Camps. I understand trying to provide jobs for the people we had helped years ago in another war, but a lot of the jobs they were performing, we already have soldiers trained for. But this would be the first of many questions I and my brothers would ask in regards to the politics of this war but for now; back to the tent.

The rest of the day would be riddled with goofing around, eating hot chow and sleeping. I ended my day with a little music from my MP3 player and got ready for whatever tomorrow would bring.

2 July 2006, started off a little earlier and a little more physical than the last couple days here. We got up, put on our full combat loads, minus ammunition, and went on a practice patrol for about 4 miles ending with a nice sprint back to the tent for some pull-ups on the make-shift bars that were made for us. By the time we got back it was getting close to chow time but I had to wait for my Driver, Caz before I could go. We were always supposed to have Battle Buddies wherever we went.

Specialist Aurelio Caz Cazares is among one of the finest soldiers I have ever had working for me. I have had a lot of great soldiers work for me in the past but he definitely makes being here very interesting and fun. He stands a little shorter than me and although a little larger than the average Stryker Driver he really knows his stuff. This guy could parallel park a Stryker in downtown New York if you asked him to and he wouldn't complain about it. He is from Texas, of Mexican Descent, he would always joke about me being an Honorary Mexican and anytime I would get pissed off or upset about something he knew how to cheer me up.

Caz wasn't even supposed to be there, he was close to getting out of the Army when he was Stop Lossed, which basically means the Army wouldn't let him out and he would be deploying with us. He never complained at all about this and although I knew it bothered him, he usually kept busy with writing letters to his family or making his way to the phones. If I could think of one title that best described Caz it would be this; Family Man. He had complete devotion to his wife and daughter and they had complete devotion to him. I think this is why he would never complain, no matter how hot or cold it was, no matter how many tires needed to be changed on the Stryker, no matter what; he would do it with a smile on his face.

3 July 2006.I started the day off with something the Army likes to call a detail. I have been given the great and honorable task of driving a bus. My reaction to receiving the detail was filled with a lot of throwing my stuff around and kicking my cot a few times but ended the same way it would end for anyone else; I drove the bus.

I would drive a small shuttle bus back and forth from the tent to the chow hall, and other places around the Camp, such as the phone center or the PX. The great thing about this job is that I am constantly in an air conditioned vehicle and I don't have to walk to the chow hall any more. I wasn't the only one with the job either so I didn't feel like a complete douche bag.

Although I was driving around in the bus most of the day I could already tell that my body was getting used to the heat again. I remember being back home watching soldiers In Iraq and Afghanistan walking in the heat of the day with all their gear and wondering how I could ever do what they are doing without dying of heat stroke, but soon we would all be back to the physical condition that we were last deployment. Soon, we will be able to throw a couple extra hundred pounds on our backs and move around the villages and cities without any problems as long as we stayed hydrated.

Hydration was key to survival in a place like this. As quickly as you can get the water in your system, the hot sun begins to suck it out of you. I remember day after day, constantly grabbing as many bottles of water as I could get just to turn around and drink them almost all at once. There were a few soldiers, however, that didn't like the idea of drinking so much water and liked to drink more soda than anything else. For most of them they would learn the hard way that water was vital, but some of them never did. They could drink a couple cases of Coke a day and be just fine. I was not one of those men.

4 July 2006, Independence Day. The entire company geared up to go to the Range. I have always found it a little interesting to have a range set up so far away from the Camp because once you get out there its nothing but desert. There is a long line of targets set up for each soldier to zero their weapons and get some practice. For all of us this would be one of the last times we will fire our weapons unless we were being shot at. Training and rehearsals are a vital part of training, giving us multiple scenarios and the proper reactions. The zero range is just one part of that training when each soldier and leader becomes confident that their primary weapons are accurate and ready to kill.

We would spend several hours at the range before returning to the Camp to our tents thinking we would be able to take our gear off and relax but the Strykers are coming in from port. No break today, not even for Independence Day. But, in the midst of all the work and preparation we have to accomplish today, it is still in the back of our minds that we are here for a purpose. Today our families back home are celebrating Independence Day by lighting fireworks and quietly thanking their sons and daughters who are here where we are for their freedom. They are the family and friends that make all of this worth it.

The Country is full of people who hate their country. They are constantly protesting and marching in our Capital because they don't agree with this war. They call us Baby Killers as we are walking through the airports in our uniforms and look away when they realize we heard them. And even though we know they hate us, we still fight. Every day we spend in country is a day that we know may be our last and we do it all for our people.

We will battle to the death knowing that all we have at this time is each other and the support of those who appreciate their freedom instead of taking advantage of it. It's hard to look in the news and see groups of Americans protesting soldier's funerals, and we still do our jobs without hesitation.

For a lot of us we consider this place home. When we are here we are in our comfort zone and when we are back in the States we are thinking about being here. No one will ever really understand it unless they have been where we are. I always love running into Veterans of past wars and listening to their stories and experiences and although we are so many years apart we are so much the same person. This job isn't for everyone including a lot of the people that make up the Army but we are here. Nothing can change that fact whether we want to be here or not, we are sworn to defend our Constitution and the people of the United States. And we will do this not just for those reasons, but to ensure the safe return of our soldiers and our brothers-in-arms here with us today. That is our Independence Day and this day will be no different for us than any other day we will spend in Kuwait and even as we head north.

1 July 2006, and a few days have passed. Not a whole lot has happened except that I have reenlisted for another couple years on top of my current contract. I didn't get much of a bonus but what I did get, I stuffed into a separate bank account because even though I have been making all this hazard pay, my bank account seems to stay fairly empty.

The intensity is as thick as the sand storm we have been having for the last 5 days. Before stepping out of the tent, I fasten my top up to my neck and cover my mouth and nose with a rag and secure goggles over my eyes. But it's so bad that the sand still manages to make its way into my lungs and I fear that I will be clearing it out of my system for months to come.

Once again we have changed plans, though. Instead of going to FOB Summerall like we were supposed to we got the word we would be heading right into the heart of the fight; Baghdad. We are to load our Strykers up on flat-bed trucks to be driven by local contractors across the border as we fly to our destination. This is a huge difference from our first deployment when we actually drove the Strykers into Iraq all the way up North to Mosul. This would be a much faster and safer way of getting all of us to our destination the only question was, would our vehicles make it?

As we are packing what gear we wouldn't be taking on the plane onto the Strykers, Caz and a lot of the other HQ guys lend us a helping hand. We are a pretty tight group consisting of a few guys that have been labeled rejects by the rest of the Company. I would never really consider myself a reject and not everyone in HQ platoon were rejects but we all had our special skills that set us apart from everyone else.

We were a mix of arms room NCOs, communications, clerks, and various jobs in the Company that play an important role in making our unit operate like a well-oiled machine. Caz and I were different because we got to be in the fight while a lot of the others would stay in the rear and keep the logistics working to keep us alive. But in the midst of them, as in any other unit, were those soldiers that were only there to collect a bigger pay check. They were part of the Fobbit club, labeled oxygen thieves. But as useless as they really were, they were still soldiers and they were still here pulled away from their families and loved ones too so we kept them as much a part of this as possible.

All the familiar faces and new faces alike, we were about to begin a year in Iraq. No matter how much experience we had, we still had no idea what to expect. There was a mixture of excitement, happiness, nervousness and even a bit of fear. We take our last moments in Kuwait to call home and stare at pictures of our families and then push it all down deep in our hearts to make room for everything we are about to experience. We are now ready for Round 2.

CHAPTER 3
Back Again

6 August 2006, we have been in Baghdad for a couple weeks now and once again Charlie Company gets the crap end of the stick. We have been put up in platoon sized tents in an area known as Tent City. Our area is surrounded by large concrete walls, but there is no overhead cover. We can walk out of our tents and look out and see the city right over the wall and we have been told that no American soldiers have been in that area for a long time so we already know that the enemy is right on the other side of those walls and we are definitely within mortar range.

We have already had the chance to make our way around FOB Liberty and check out what this place has to offer. The chow hall is fairly close for a change, and the PX is right across the road from there. But what we have seen in front of the PX is so odd that it makes us wonder when we will be forced to leave this FOB. There is a Burger King here and the Whopper Burgers are amazing. There is air conditioning in nearly every little building here so we only have to suffer the heat for a few minutes at a time.

Our Company CP (Command Post) is just past the chow hall and we have already begun setting it up for future operations. The motor pool is quite a walk from the tents and as a vehicle crew, Caz and I have already made several trips there to check and recheck our Strykers. All day and night we can here the prayers just outside the walls from the many large mosque towers and they are usually followed by the familiar sounds of incoming mortar rounds that have yet to hit near us.

There is an old familiar smell in the air that I wish I could have forgotten, but this is the type of thing that can never be forgotten. The majority of the city's sewage runs out of houses and into the alley ways and the smell is a mixture of crap, burning trash and death. If there is one thing I will never forget leaving this place, it's the freaking smell.

Finally, we have been able to get outside the FOB and get started on our patrols in the city. A big part of being here is starting off with a show of force. The last time we were here, the Strykers struck fear into the hearts of the Iraqis however, this time is different. They are used to us and they are ready for us and have made a lot of changes to the way they fight us. The streets are an ever-changing mass of IEDs although we go days without seeing them, some days that is all we see. There are several ways to hide an IED; they can be hidden in cars, dead animals, ditches, trees, power lines, culverts and a lot of the bigger bombs are buried right under the streets. The first day out and 2nd and 3rd Platoons have already been hit with smaller IEDs. Luckily no casualties, just a lot of headaches.

Finding the IEDs is a long painful process consisting of VCs scanning the roads with the RWS (remote weapon station) which sits on top of the Stryker as the main weapon system. The RWS has two types of cameras on it which allows the VC to sit inside the vehicle and scan for targets under protection of the vehicles armor. One of these cameras, known as the TIM (Thermal Imaging Module) has the ability to detect heat which a lot of IEDs will have a unique heat signature which allows us to sometimes see them before it's too late.

If we suspect an IED near-by we stop movement and set up security and call for a separate unit to come and dispose of it. This process can take anywhere from twenty minutes to five or six hours which leaves us open for enemy attacks and Snipers. Sadly, however they are usually found when a friendly unit sets them off which usually ends with injury or even the loss of a fellow brother.

Today we got to execute a fairly decent patrol and we even got to visit the infamous Green Zone. I like to think of it as the Disneyland of Iraq. There are a lot of Saddam monuments and old buildings and palaces in this area and it is the place to be if you are stationed here. We stop at a popular monument called The Hands of Victory which was built to celebrate the defeat of Iran. It consists of two large joining hands, said to be Saddams hands, and is the entrance to a large parade ground. At the base of the monument are several Iranian helmets that have been pressed into the concrete.

We take the time for a lot of photos of each other before loading back up and heading back to the FOB. For the most part this has been almost like a vacation aside from a couple of small IEDs.

August 2006 was another rough day for the Battalion. Alpha Company rolled their second Stryker, our 2nd Platoon took another IED disabling the whole Stryker and wounding one Squad Leader, SSG Hansen, who took some debris in his face. HHC (Headquarters and Headquarters Company) wasn't so lucky, however, when two of the Battalion Snipers were wounded in a drive by.

Their first trip out and SSG Brady, who used to be in my

Company, was shot in the leg from an AK-47, taking a large chunk of meat from his thigh. Also wounded in the attack was SPC Flannery, another former Comanche who was hit in the hand losing a tip of his finger and literally exploding the magazine on his rifle. Both of them will survive, but will most likely be out of the fight for a while if not the rest of the deployment.

SSG Brady, a more stocky guy, was one of those guys that if he had your back you could get away with anything. I remember nights at the barracks, before I was married, and Brady would be out on the balcony with nothing but a shaving cream bikini on screaming at everyone in the parking lot. He is a bit of a hillbilly, and along with a small group of friends would always be causing some kind of ruckus.

I got the pleasure of becoming friends with him and we started a tradition called Bon Fuego in which every Saturday night we would rob wooden pallets from the local Shopette on Fort Lewis and head out into the woods near a lake to a secret location. Along the route we would lay out chem. Lights and tell only the people we wanted there to follow the chem. Lights and once we had a full crowd we would go pick them up so no one could find us.

The rest of the night would be a full night of drinking and playing country music as loud as possible and somewhere in the night I would usually bring out my guitar and we would all sing some old Garth Brooks songs. This tradition would carry on for a long time until other units got wind of it and started crashing the party, eventually fading them away. There are still whispers of these parties to this day. But, Brady and Flannery were injured while I was on my second patrol.

Patrols are pretty regular now, the Platoons have their own rotations and HQ platoon is a mixture of my crew and other crews from the Tanker and Mortar sections. Our Unit is different in that we are not just a Company full of regular grunts. We have Sniper, Mortar, Tanker and FSO sections as well, and we have molded them into a sort of 4th Platoon. In the 4th Platoon we have a usual patrol that takes us to the local Iraqi Police Station to try and get information on the mix of local Sunni and Shea Muslims living in the area.

The two have been fighting for many years and we are trying to find out who the bad guys really are and gather information from the local police on suspected dirty cops within their own organization. This has proven to be a long and painful process because if they are not dirty, then they are afraid to say who it for fear that they will lose their own lives as well as their families.

In this neighborhood if you are the wrong type of Muslim or a Christian you are in danger. Hajj will sneak into your house in the middle of the night and take you from your bed and execute you in a secure location then dump your body on the streets or in an alley somewhere. This was an everyday sight for us and we regularly had to stop patrols and report the body to the local police to come and pick them up. We would find these bodies with their hands and feet tied together and a rag or a sack over their heads.

Sometimes the bodies would be used to hide small IEDs to injure any soldiers that would investigate the body and in turn lose his life as well. We always had to be careful when finding any of them because of this reason, however the local police had no fear of this happening to them and would back their police trucks up to the body and load them up in the back and we would continue on with our patrol like it was another day in the office.

This sort of Ethnic Cleansing happened every day here in this neighborhood and it was a common sight for us to drive in to the local police station and see a few of these victims laying around covered in flies. We were so used to it that we got to the point where the sight and smell would not even bother us and would continue gathering the information we needed while standing right next to them.

As I came back in from my patrol another group was headed out. Among the group were a few HQ guys, SSG Ewing, SGT Doherty, and SPC Doranski. I considered them my friends, some more than others, but as they were out and I was recovering from my patrol I actually got a chance to sit and think about Brady and Flannery, hoping they were ok. I started to wonder about my friends that were out at the time and wonder if they were next. Was it going to be my turn the next time I was out?

SSG Ewing, or Mikey, as we called him, a skinny country boy in Tanker section was in charge of the two other guys, Doherty and Doranski. Doherty was a veteran of the last deployment, but his tour was cut short due to a tragedy back home and had to return early. A fairly mouthy guy from Boston, he always liked to talk crap to whoever was around and had an extensive collection of porn on his computer that seemed to grow on a daily basis.

SPC Gary Doranski, a large Polish guy, from Missouri was a tough, but quiet guy. He was an alternate driver for my crew and would switch out with my driver, Caz every once in a while to get some time out of the wire. We always talked about being back home in Missouri because we were from similar home towns which kind of set us apart from everyone else, except for a few other guys that were also from Missouri including our Company Commander, CPT Matthew Pike.

CPT Pike was a tough but fair Commander and I enjoyed being his VC. Every time we left for a patrol I would have my MP3 player hooked into the vehicles intercom system and we would roll out listening to the same song. Coming back into the wire was a great feeling followed with the song, Mad World by Gary Jules and we would just keep quiet and enjoy the song as we rolled through the gates to safety. It was these traditions among others that helped us keep our sanity during the inevitable crap that we would go through on a daily basis.CPT Pike was very strong with tradition and would not even allow anyone else to VC or drive his Stryker for fear that t change could bring tragedy.

CPT Pike was also a passionate bird watcher and would on many occasions take a quick break from a patrol to point out such birds as the Hooded Crow, explaining each bird in detail to us. Once on the FOB, if there was nothing going on, he would take off with his camera and binoculars and come back with tons of pictures from a day of bird watching. It is amazing to me how unique each person in this Company really is and how we all come together will always remain a mystery to me, but we did and no one could ever take that from us.

1August 2006 a long and drawn out day on an MSR (Main Supply Route).My Stryker, along with the Tanker section patrolled out and down Route Sword in search for possible IEDs. Route Sword was the sort of road that would seem like the typical 4 lane highway to the average American. However, along this route were countless amounts of IEDs hidden away waiting for a US or Iraqi patrol and every time we drove the route we could see evidence of a burned up vehicle and often would have to stop for possible sightings.

We were supposed to be heading north to a possible hot spot for IEDs and also to drop off the Snipers to over watch our movement but we were blocked on the route by a supply convoy and stopped by our Bravo Company with a suspected IED. We sat for a bit and set up security until the convoy was clear. One of our gunners spotted a heat signature on the side of the road and part of the procedure was to call it up to higher.

Higher, consisted of a few guys manning the Battalion radios back on the FOB and often enough were either unreliable or couldn't get us what we needed to get the job done. They would watch with their unmanned planes in the sky and tell us where to go and what to do even though we were here on the ground and knew exactly what sort of threat we had been facing. This posed a problem on many occasions and today was no different.

I plotted our position and called it up to the battalion requesting for EOD (Explosives Ordnance Disposal) to come and investigate. This process had the potential of taking forever because our higher had to call it up to their higher to get permission to request EOD. Then, if we actually got EOD we had to wait until they were available which could take forever sometimes. Today was one of those days and we sat on the MSR for several hours in a very bad position to be.

Along with being in the middle of a large open area, we were right at the end of a place called RPG alley.RPG (Rocket Propelled Grenade) alley was a long open area to the North of us that often would be used as an attack position for convoys that moved through the area. It was also a great place for a Sniper to hide as our Platoon Leader, Lt Rogers, would find out that day.

As we sat there everyone in the patrol would end up fighting over stupid crap because we were all tired and we were all hot. Everyone knew the threat of being where we were and Lt Rogers was beginning to get pissed at them. Lt Rogers was a strong religious man, but knew what it took to be a fighter. He was fairly new, but had enough experience to know that we were in a bad spot. However bad it was, Battalion ordered us to stay in position to watch this IED so when EOD would actually show up we could go on about our business.

As we sat there, LT Rogers was standing up out of his hatch when suddenly I heard a loud bang on the side of the Stryker. A sniper had taken a shot at Lt Rogers and luckily missed. I immediately pulled LT Rogers down into the vehicle, which hadn't heard the shot but knew to keep down once I told him what I heard. We sat there for a couple hours when Battalion finally called us.

Comanche 66, this is Tomahawk X-Ray be advised you are sitting next to a possible IED location. These were the words that came across our battalion radio, and we couldn't believe our ears. I was pretty pissed at that point and called back. Roger, this is Comanche 66 Tango; we are the ones that called that IED to you. do you have any information on EODs location?

The Battalion radio guard had done a shift change and the guys that left didn't brief them of our current situation so they had no idea that we had been on that road for so long waiting for support. They said that EOD wouldn't leave without a better description of the potential bomb, which we had already called up to Battalion hours ago. It was at this moment where I had first lost my cool and shouted back at them, Tomahawk X-Ray; you need to work on your freaking battle hand-overs because we called in this IED hours ago with a full description You said they were coming! LT Rogers took over the radio for me because I was sick of dealing with those morons. He was a lot better at keeping his cool than I was.

After a while longer the decision was made to investigate closer and we found that the heat signature in the road turned out to be nothing. All that for nothing, but that is how it works in this day and age. With the amount of casualties we take every day from IEDs it's good to be cautious instead of rushing into it and getting killed. But mix a nervous gunner with inexperience and you also have the potential of getting caught up in an ambush and that never turned out good. This was the first time in Iraq where I started to realize that I may not make it home alive.

13 August 2006, was the start of The Surge of Baghdad. President Bush ordered over 20,00more troops to deploy to Iraq and we were kicking off what would be a very long mission.

Each Battalion was assigned sectors in the Capital City and we were to basically start from one end of our sector and clear all the way across. As simple as this sounds, combine an entire Brigade of Infantry with Strykers and add in the Iraqi Army and local police. The mission was supposed to be a joint effort but ended up being more of a babysitting job for us to watch the Iraqi Army because they were using the mission to get into rival

Muslims and Christians homes and harass them.

The Iraqi Army wasn't very well trained either and would often accidentally fire their weapons inside homes and vehicles. This was happening when we had our backs turned and once again we were fighting the Religious Politic battle trying to balance peace with both sides.

I wasn't in my Stryker for this mission, instead the CPT Pike pulled me and a few others from the crew to dismount and walk among the Company while they cleared. I was carrying the radio on my back to keep in contact with the Battalion HQ and keep them up to speed with what we were doing. It was during this mission that we were starting to see how much training a lot of the other HQ guys needed on the ground. They were used to being on the vehicles and now they were on the ground in full kits in 113 degree weather. We had guys dropping left and right from dehydration but I was doing fine.

I got my Infantry roots in this unit before we had Strykers and spent a lot of time walking with as much weight on my back as possible; however towards the end of the mission it was starting to wear on me.

Just to bury a myth, we didn't have air conditioned Strykers so all the crap we got from other units for having it easier was just a bunch of bullcrap. And even though I was a VC I was on the ground a lot of the time that everyone else was on the ground. We had to be well trained as VCs but we also had to be flexible whenever we were needed on the ground.

It was during these next few days that we had found a significantly large cache of weapons and explosives in the more secluded areas in our sector.

2August 2006, I was back on my Stryker with CPT Pike, Caz, SGT Nathan Reider (The Battalion Commo) and SSG Arthur Foster.

SGT Nathan Reider, an average sized guy with a not so average view of the world. He wasn't an angry person by any means but if he was mad everyone knew about it because he was the voice of the Company Commander on the radio. He was attached to our Company as our Communications NCO and was on the ground with CPT Pike when one of our Platoons discovered a decent sized cache. Our Stryker was left in an over watch position near the cache.

The plan was to sit there and wait for EOD to come and

dispose of the cache, which from past experience could turn out to be a very long weight and it was especially hot.SSG Arthur Foster and I along with my driver, Caz were sitting in the vehicle waiting for news so we could get out of area and back to our tent.

As the hours went by we were starting to run out of water and the ice we packed was completely melted. We were calling in resupply from other Companies who were already leaving the sector so they dropped all they could at our vehicle.SSG Foster, a stockier guy was fairly new to HQ Platoon and was assigned as our Platoon Sergeant. A huge fan of the Green Bay Packers, he was the target of a lot of our jokes and would often get upset at us but always had a joke to fire back at us. His least favorite joke was when we called him, Bobble Head because he had a large head.

I remember when he first came to the Platoon, not many of us liked him because right away he established his ground as The Man and tried to make our section into something that a lot of these guys weren't ready for. As the bastard children our section was full of guys who could care less for the mission, but he tried to make them care. On this day the group of us on the Stryker that day became a little bit closer and Foster would become part of the team in a lot of ways.

We finally got more water, EOD showed up to detonate the cache and we all returned to the FOB as different people all together. It's strange to think that you know a man for what he seems to be like until you serve with him in a combat zone and then you become more of a brother than you ever were before.

CHAPTER 4
Dan and Kenney

27 August 2006 will be a day that lives in the hearts of our Company forever. I along with a group of guys from our section was recovering from the previous days patrols when CPT Pike came into the tent in a bit of a hurry and told us to get a group of guys together and load up on the Stryker. He told us that one of the 3rd Platoon Strykers had been hit by a large IED and there were casualties.

We immediately geared up not saying a word to each other and quickly ran to the motor pool. I remember everything that was going through my head at the time and it was a mixture of mental checks that Caz and I had everything we needed and fear of what may be happening to our brothers still out there. We quickly started up the vehicle and powered up the RWS and rushed to the Company CP to pick up CPT Pike and our First Sergeant, 1SG Mcclin.

We met up with the other vehicles that would roll out with us and headed north towards a familiar sector off or Route Sword. As we moved closer to RPG Alley we could see smoke from the Stryker that had been hit and we could see American Humvees on the side of the road pulling bodies out of Iraqi vehicles and laying them outside by side. The bodies were covered in blood from what looked like a lot of gun fire and the vehicles had a small amount of smoke coming from bullet riddled holes in the sides. I remember driving past a shoe in the middle of the road as we pulled onto the scene of the attack.

C32, the 2nd Squad Stryker of our 3rd Platoon was laying on its side and several feet behind it was a large crater in the road filled with water. Insurgents had placed a very large IED under the street next to a water main and as C32 drove over it the bomb detonated tossing several pieces of armor high into the air and tossing a couple of the soldiers out of the rear air guard hatches onto the street behind the vehicle.

The VC, CPL Kenneth Cross was killed in the attack and the driver, PVT Dan Dolan was still pinned inside his driver's hole. The squad was extremely shook up as they franticly raced to get him out of the badly damaged Stryker.CPT Pike moved us into position facing down a small alley as he dismounted to investigate while the 1SG and I pulled security.

I immediately began monitoring Company and Battalion NET to gather as much information as I could get and almost as soon as we arrived on scene we began to here mortar impacts not far from our position. I scanned about 20meters down the alley as the 1SG and I spotted a small van racing towards us from the end of the alley. As pissed off as we were we immediately took aim and as soon as the driver saw my M2 .50cal machine gun bear down on him he slammed on the breaks and slowly turned around. He was almost at the wrong place at the wrong time.

Large recovery vehicles arrived on scene and a few hours later had the Stryker loaded on to a flat bed truck as CPT Pike and a few other leaders were knocking on doors and asking questions to everyone living near the scene. I remember feeling so much hate and anger at the local people and ready to just shoot any person that looked at me wrong, but I had to stay focused. I couldn't let my 1SG or my driver think that I was going to lose my cool even though I am sure they were feeling the same way. Besides, I had to think about 3rd Platoon and what they were going through. We knew that they had lost one brother and another was badly injured.

For Infantry Companies everyone has a click. Each Platoon stuck together but in a Company like this all the Stryker Crew Members had their own special bonds that were usually shared as we passed by each other in the chow hall or met up at the fuel point after a patrol. I remember just a few days ago Caz and I pulled up behind Cross and Dolans Stryker after a mission and since we had loud air horns on our vehicles we didn't hesitate to blast it at them while they were trying to fuel up. Dolan was on top of the Stryker while Cross was fueling up and they immediately started laughing as they flipped us off and carried on about their business. This was a regular thing for all of the crews and as we would all stage at the ice point before a mission, while the squads would go get a quick bite at the chow hall, all the crews would meet up and joke around before moving out. This was the bond that we shared on a daily basis.

As much as we didn't want to believe what was happening we all accepted this as war and this was the first day that we had experienced a loss in our Company. Each member of the Platoon was accomplishing their mission and was working their asses off to save PVT Dolan from the wreck without even thinking about their own injuries. Several of the squad was badly injured and the evacuation process began shortly when PVT Dolan was finally freed from the wreck.

I remember about this time someone from one of the Battalion Humvees called up to report that one of their crew was suffering from heat exhaustion and was requesting medical assistance.CPT Pike was back on the Stryker at the time, but I still had control of the radios. I remember passing that Humvee as we rolled on to the scene and recalled seeing an air conditioner unit on it. I began to get pissed because the soldier in particular was a very heavy set man and rarely left the wire and I was sure that he had not been drinking water. I responded with, Don't you have air conditioned Humvees? Move him into the cool air and give him some water, the medics are busy! CPT Pike immediately took over and told me to be careful what I say on the NET and even though this was a tense situation there was no need to get crazy. He was right, so I went back to scanning my area and a few hours later we were headed back to the FOB.

I remember the trip back and not a soul on the Stryker said a word as we cleared our weapons inside the gate of the FOB. We returned to our tents shook up and a little scared for Cross and Dolans family and also 3rd Platoon. We all lay down on our cots at the end of it all and even though I was tired I knew I wouldn't sleep that night. Hours past until 2345 hours that night SSG Ewing knelt beside my cot and told me that PVT Dolan had died during surgery from his wounds. I closed my eyes and for the first time in a long time I began to pray. I prayed for them, their families, their brothers in 3rd Platoon and I prayed that our Company would remain strong and be able to push through this and continue to fight. Today every member of our Company opened their eyes to the reality of what we were here for and every one of us wanted payback.

1 September 2006, we think we caught em. Early this morning our Company conducted a raid on a neighborhood and caught a couple guys on the list. The List refers to a Black List of known terrorists, crooked cops and other members of terrorist organizations. We used checked this list any time we caught any one and would usually detain them to gather information when possible.

These guys had maps and digital imagery on them and tested positive for traces of TNT. We had the technology to check anyone for traces of certain substances like explosives or bomb making materials. Supposedly the IED that hit C32, killing CPL Cross and PVT Dolan, was initiated by command wire meaning someone waited for them to drive over the bomb before detonating it. This command wire was found running to a house where the men were detained.

We rolled to the target house about 0430 hours and immediately spotted military aged males on the roof of the target building. They looked scared and I had a couple of them in the reticule on my RWS just waiting for an excuse. Usually about this time a night if someone was spotted on a roof top they were either sleeping in the cool air of the night, or they were planning on something completely different. We had to treat each mission as if they were waiting to ambush us but would not open fire unless there was a definite threat. My Stryker and a few others were set in an over watch position across the street well out of site as we watched members of 3rd Platoon move to the house and set explosive breaches on the doors.

One the main advantages of being a Stryker VC is that I have access to the Thermal Sites on the RWS. With this site I can easily watch anything with a heat signature move around. I took great pride in the fact that I could track someone, enemy or not, from several hundred meters away and they would have no idea that I was watching them. The thought that I could squeeze the trigger at any second and they would never even know that I was there made me feel like I had complete control over their fate. I used to think in my head every time I was watching a suspicious person that I am the last face that they will never see.

This night however the squads on the ground got to have all the fun as explosions rocked the area and I could see our boys going straight into the target house so quickly that before the last man was in the door they were already calling up to us that they had detained two suspects.

I can't imagine what they were feeling knowing that they may have just captured the very men responsible for the death of their two brothers, but they were very professional about it and stuck to the plan. They had to trust that once the detainees were brought back to the holding all the right questions would be asked and that there would be some retribution for their pain. I am sure that it was very difficult to hold back as they loaded them onto their Strykers but we were different than the enemy. We were Comanche Company and we didn't sink to their level.

We all returned back to the FOB hopeful that justice would take its course but we didn't have time to think about it because we needed to rest. Tonight would be the memorial service for CPL Cross and PVT Dolan and it was time to say good bye.

Before the memorial service I reported to the chapel because I was to help with the ceremony. As I walked into the sanctuary I immediately saw that the platform had already been built. At the front of the church were two rifles secured facing the floor on two bayonets. Atop the butt stock of the rifles were helmets and the dog tags of Cross and Dolan hung from the handles of them. At the base of the platform were photographs of the two soldiers, one of Cross with his wife and Dolan next to a Stryker. Around the platform were different medals that they would be awarded for their actions and a couple pairs of desert boots were standing at the position of attention.

I had to look away as I gazed across the pictures and even though I closed my eyes I could still see their faces, goofing off at the fuel point, dancing and singing in the tents in Kuwait, and many other memories that I have had the pleasure of keeping in my mind. Even though we weren't in the same Platoon I still looked at them as brothers and if it was this difficult for me, how much harder it would be for those that were lucky enough to serve shoulder to shoulder with them.

The Memorial began as any other memorial would and followed with friends and leaders sharing experiences with the two brothers and I watched as 3rd Platoon stood up to say their final good byes as the 21 Gun salute rang out from outside the chapel. As Taps played each of us had a heavy heart and no matter how tough we thought we were I will always remember looking over and seeing grown men cry. The toughest men on the face of the planet were mourning the loss of two great warriors and with all the training and all the hardening the Army has put into them nothing could stop their tears from falling.

Each member of the Platoon lined up in front of the memorial and saluted to say their final good byes, followed by leadership and anyone else in the Chapel that wanted to pay their respects. At the end of the service our Brigade Commander pulled us all together in the chapel and summed up the whole experience in one line; It never gets easier.

CHAPTER 5
Motor Pool Guard

8 September 2006, and I have tried this entire time to not have to pull Motor Pool Guard but, eventually, most of us have to do it. Caz and I have it from 050to 090hours so the temperature isn't so bad. I have taken the post by myself as Caz has gone for a chow run. The motor pool isn't so far from tent city; however, it is pretty far from the chow hall so I would expect him to be gone for a while. I have decided to bring a book by Nietzsche with me and try to get a little culture in this crap hole of a country.

The city has been fairly quiet lately, not a lot of gun fire and just the random IEDs being disposed of by EOD. It's exciting to know that the Sweepers are succeeding along such busy routes. The Sweepers, as I like to call them, are a long convoy of EOD bomb hunters and when they find an IED they set explosives on them with robots. The crapppy thing about it is there is usually no warning when they decide to detonate and the explosions can be rather large. When we hear the explosions everyone pauses for a moment, wondering if that was EOD or if someone got hit.

Yesterday morning, The Sweepers, found an EFP (Explosively Formed Projectile).EFPs are a new weapon evolved from the IED that contains a shaped charged piece of metal that when detonated can tear through almost any armor. An EFP can tear through a Stryker hull like it was hot butter and is often detonated near the engine or squad leader area damaging the armor and often ripping through the troops inside. This is how the war has adapted over the last few years; we get new and better equipment and Hajj figures out a way to beat it. Even the smallest of EFPs can be lethal and I have seen smaller ones rip through the hull, the engine block and back through the other side of the Stryker. You could actually look through one side and see daylight at the other end.

As soon as this shift is over I am probably going to try and get a work out in before lying down.SGT Reider and myself started lifting weights in Kuwait to help pass the time and to get in shape. We had gotten some diet and work-out plans from some friends of ours and we seemed to be making pretty good progress. We were both fairly average sized guys almost at the same strength level so we were constantly challenging each other.

Lifting weights was something that we could do to escape the realities of this place and this is probably why people in prison lift weights besides the obvious excuse that they had to be tougher than the next guy. It wasn't much different here because I have been on patrols where I have had to gain control over an Iraqi that was twice my size.

Every week we would take a day in the gym and lift as much as we could to track our progress. I could tell that I was getting bigger eating as much protein and carbs that I could get at the chow hall along with a lot of Protein drinks before and after work-outs.

We started in Kuwait barely able to lift 16pounds and now we were lifting 235 pounds. This may not sound like much but we were pretty proud of it. We had a gym set right outside of our tent and took advantage of this as much as possible. Regardless if I ever worked out at all nothing could change the fact that no one returns home from war weaker.

11 September 2006, marks the 5 year anniversary of the brutal attacks on the Twin Towers in New York. We had a moment to reflect on where we were and what we were feeling when we were given the news that our Country had been viciously attacked by terrorists.

I was on maneuver range training back in Fort Lewis and back then I was a Specialist. I will never forget when our Company Commander, then CPT JC Glick, and First Sergeant Rodriguez stopped our training exercise and brought the whole Company together and sat us down. He said to us in a quiet yet tough voice, Men, we have been attacked. The World Trade Center in New York City is no longer standing. The First Sergeant had secured a TV and VCR to playback the footage from the Twin Towers and we watched, devastated at what we were seeing. We were given the opportunity to call from cellular phones to family if we had any in New York or the Pentagon and not even a few minutes later we were getting geared back up to continue training.

In our minds we had been pushed by some evil force and we wanted to push back. So this training took on a whole new attitude and anger and determination motivated us to get ready for what we knew would be war. As we pushed forward on imaginary and wooden targets you could hear the battle cries for miles as we fired our weapons, pretending that we were taking the heads off of an enemy that we had never even seen.

I remember one soldier in particular who stopped in the

middle of the mission and sat down in the middle of the range. He decided that he didn't want to be a part of our Army any longer and claimed that he wanted to quit. Almost immediately he was pulled away by team leaders and squad leaders and taken into the wood line for a little pep talk. In the end, the soldier refused to train and we got to see our first casualty of war even though we had never set foot on a battle ground.

Now five years later, we were right in the middle of a war zone for a second time and 9/11 is a distant memory to us and no matter what political views we had or what theories each of us shared about that day, nothing could change the fact that we were here and we had a mission. Each day since then we have gotten some form of pay back one way or another but it will never erase what happened.

12 September 2006, Last night I pulled a muscle in my neck, during a mission, so I have spent most of the day laid out trying to get my flexibility back. The mission was a success, however, and the Iraqi Police and Iraqi Army have finally started working together. We were to conduct three big hits on known Insurgents and pull over watch for the local forces to get in the different target houses and get the bad guys.

We secured outer perimeters and watched as they quickly grabbed each target and the entire raid took about 45 minutes total. We were back in the wire by 0100 hours and were able to make it back in time for Midnight Chow. As we were eating in the parking lot we could hear the awesome sounds of Delta and Rangers conducting a near-by hit on what I suspect a very important target. One of the assets they had at their disposal was a C-130 Specter Gunship and they were raining down hell on somebody. They were in our area of operations but we couldn't do anything about it so we just looked on.

The Specter Gunship is an amazing plane that can drop a lot of lethal bombs or bullets on a target. If you look at it at night through NVGs (Night Vision Goggles) you can see a beam of light shining from the plane to the targets below. We called this beam of light The Finger of God because anything it touched could either remain unharmed or completely obliterated in an instant. This sort of fire power was more than just a killing tool, but also a great way to use show of force. I had a smile on my face that night just knowing that we were killing something or someone.

2September 2006, the last few days have kicked up a bit of excitement in a few different ways.3rd Platoon was hit again by a Sniper this time and had wounded one of the younger soldiers, PVT Bratager. He wasn't seriously wounded but the round had hit him in his communications head set and bounced down to his collar. Although he was very lucky he will have a nice scar for the rest of his life to remind him just how lucky he was. I remember joking with him after the incident telling him he should write the company that made the head set and get some sort of royalties because it saved his life. He could at least get a new head set.

Sniper attacks were getting a little more common in the war these days. Hajj was finding new ways to hide including removing tail lights from the back of a parked car and using one hole to fire out of and the other hole for a video camera to record the kill. After each kill the enemy sniper would collect them all up and use them as propaganda against us on the internet. This process was done for more than just sniper kills, though, and even after C32 was hit by an IED we could see the video on the internet and was able to use this footage to find the location of where they were hiding. Of course this came too late but we were starting to learn from this footage exactly how they were doing things.

One Iraqi Sniper, commonly known as Juba, had made several propaganda videos protesting us as Infidels and often would make threats on President Bush. Some considered him a myth or legend but we didn't care either way. Somewhere out there were highly trained snipers who could hide pretty much any where they wanted and were killing more and more soldiers every day. They could place themselves in the middle of crowded streets, take out a target and move out before anyone realized where they were.

We were slowly seeing Strykers rolling around with large camouflage nets on the top which made them look like rolling houses. I remember making fun of them but this new tactic was working because even though we could see out enough to pull security, Hajj could not see us leaving him no choice but to spray and pray. The Stryker, however, was beginning to take on extra weight and they were breaking down even faster with all the new protective devices we were slapping on them.

Our mission yesterday did not require any sort of cammo netting on top or extra protection, however we could have used a few extra sets of wire cutters when we were tasked with Engineer escort. We moved into a farm area and pulled security as a group of Engineers were moving barriers around to control traffic along the route.

About midway through the mission we spotted a large fire ball shoot up into the sky approximately 40meters away. I quickly scanned the area with the RWS and spotted three individuals running from the scene of the explosion. I could not get a positive ID on them and did not get permission to engage due to the fact that they may have been just scared farmers running away.

We could hear from the information we were gathering from the Battalion NET that a car bomb had exploded at an Iraqi check point and we quickly loaded up to go investigate the attack. As we loaded up we could hear a lot of small arms fire and could tell it was AK-47s.I looked around me to see a few of the Engineers were hiding near their trucks for fear that they would be attacked also and we had to motivate them to load up so we could leave.

We finally got ready to move out and my Stryker was moving behind a large mound of dirt when we felt the vehicle suddenly start to slow down. I was scanning with the RWS so LT Rogers was guiding Caz around various obstacles, however, we ended up getting caught up in some concertina wire left there by other forces in the past. I was furious as I quickly called up other vehicles to send dismounts to my vehicle and check to seriousness of our predicament.

We were pretty we wrapped up and would need a couple sets of wire cutters to free us from the web of sharp wire and a lot of time would be wasted as I continued to scan. We kept in contact with the Company CP, careful not to let them know what we were going through but we were stuck and couldn't get to the Iraqi checkpoint for at least another 2minutes.

Finally, we were free and all the dismounts were loaded up and we raced to the scene of the car bomb. As we arrived we could see the damage and several pieces of what looked like a four door car were scattered all over the highway. After asking some questions we found that only a couple Iraqi soldiers were wounded and no one was killed. We were relieved and yet we were laughing our asses when we realized how freaking stupid that suicide bomber would be feeling to know that the only person he actually killed was himself. As I scanned the surrounding areas I started to remember a day from my first deployment.

We were stationed at a little COP (Combat Outpost) called, COP Blickenstaff, right in the heart of downtown Mosul. Our COP was surrounded by a very large concrete wall and we had guard towers surrounding the whole thing. I was driving a little four-runner to get water for our barracks when a large explosion shook the entire area and I looked not even 10feet from the outside of the wall as a large fire ball and black smoke rose up into the sky.

We gathered up our squads and rushed outside to secure the area right outside of our back gate. A car bomb and been ignited in the middle of a busy street and every window in the surrounding buildings had been blown out along with several cars nearby that had been damaged or burned. We could see inside the cars that there were still bodies completely charred at this point. The smell was horrible and unlike anything I could ever describe and to this day I remember what it was like.

I was instructed to move to the corner of the intersection facing out to pull security and as I kneeled there I looked down beside me and saw a red chunk of meat covered in blood. It was a piece of human remains that had been thrown from the car and I remember staring at it for several minutes wondering if it was from the bomber or an innocent by-stander. I gathered my senses and went back to scanning the area and it was at that point that I realized that none of this really bothered me at all. I could stare at a thousand dead bodies and I would feel as if I was sitting at home watching TV with my feet on the coffee table.

I am no war machine by any means and if you saw me on the streets you would probably think, This guy was in a war? But, for some reason I was starting to feel comfortable here. This would all be confirmed for me over the next year or so when I returned to the states only to find myself wishing I had never come back. I wanted to stay where I was and keep fighting every day and in the middle of a blown up city street I could look around me and see a home away from home.

CHAPTER 6
Day 100

7 October 2006, today 4th Platoon and myself were headed north up to the local Iraqi Police station to investigate some suspicious cops. This route was a normally busy street that headed towards a bridge into another Company's sector. Our sectors were divided by a creek affectionately known as Shit Creek because of the horrifying smell that we could detect from hundreds of meters away at the Police Station.

I had given Caz this day off to rest and call home to his wife, so I had Doranski, whom we had now nicknamed The Polish Hammer due to the fact that he was a large, almost Sasquatch-like, guy and he was Polish. Along with me was the usual security in the rear hatches and LT Rogers who was usually the guy that would go in and talk to the Iraqi Police to gather information.

We were traveling about 35 or 4miles-per-hour when I noticed the Stryker in front of me swerve to miss a suspicious cardboard box on the left side of the road. We didn't have as much time to react as they did and as soon as we past it I felt a large blast of air and smoke hit the left-front side of the vehicle and I was knocked out.

Seconds later I regained consciousness and climbed up out of my hatch and quickly realized that we had been hit by an IED. Doranski continued to drive and I looked through the drivers hole only to see it full of smoke. He was driving blind and was not responding to me yelling for a good minute or so. Finally, he answered my calls and said he could finally start to see and we guided the vehicle past the kill zone.

LT Rogers called for me, Apes! as he always called me, I'm bleeding Look at my face! I remember thinking that I may turn to look at him and see half his face missing so I yelled back, I don't want to look at your face, sir! I was filled with a mixture of confusion, fear, and anger I looked only to see that his face was fine but his hands and arms were peppered with small pieces of shrapnel. I quickly began to check myself for wounds and that's when I realized that I could not hear out of my left ear and my shoulder was badly damaged.

LT Rogers made the call to move out of the area and get to the Police Station where we could assess the damage to the vehicle and seek medical attention. I was completely dazed but I remember looking around at people on the streets wishing that they would look at me wrong so I could cut them to pieces with my .5cal.I was severely pissed off!

As we pulled inside the walls of the Police Station I dismounted and immediately went to Doranski to see if he was ok. He was a little shook up but he was not wounded and we started to survey the damage to our Stryker. Nearly all the tires were flattened and the entire left side of the vehicle was riddled with holes and much of the armor was badly damaged. We were very lucky to be alive as any of these pieces of metal had hit us wrong and we could have been killed. I through my helmet at the ground furious and wanting to go back down the road where we were hit and proceed to mow everything down!

Inside the yard were a couple if Iraqi bodies that had been picked up by the Police and I remember walking up to them and staring them in their faces. A lot of things were going through my mind at this point and all I wanted to do was smash my boot right into their throats and scream at the top of my lungs, What the freak are we doing here?!!!I could not believe we were here in this place fighting for a country that didn't want us there. They didn't want our help and they sure as hell didn't want to start living the Democratic way of life. The only thing they wanted to do was keep killing each other in mass quantities and the messed up part of it is, a lot of the people in our own country were calling us murderers and saying that we are the ones doing all the killing over here. The only time we ever killed any Iraqi is when they were trying to kill us. period!

The Doc pulled me to the side and began to check my shoulder and could tell that it was starting to swell up pretty bad. We gathered a little information from the Iraqi Police so we didn't go back empty handed and drove the damaged Stryker back to the FOB to be repaired as much as possible by the mechanics so that we could get it back to mission capable status. I was ordered, however, to report to the Aid Station along with Doranski and a couple other guys.

The Docs there checked my ears and could see in my left ear that there was significant damage to the ear drum and canal and my shoulder had been torn and bruised in more than one place. I had a mild concussion but, I felt like a complete douche bag at this point because I had allowed the enemy to get me. Although it wasn't the worst of injuries I was already being told that I would be living with some of this damage for the rest of my life but I didn't give a crap, I just wanted to get out of there and get back to my Company.

I was finally released from the Aid Station and reported to

my Company CP and was greeted with a lot of concern from everyone there, and spotted LT Rogers who was fine and that's when we started to call each other, The Bash Brothers. I finally made my way down to the motor pool dazed and very much in pain. A large group of guys had already begun changing the tires on the Stryker and with the help of some of the guys from 4th Platoon and my crew the vehicle was already Fully Mission Capable. I went back to my tent and lay down on my cot a little shook up, but ready to get some rest.

Despite concerns from my chain of command and a lot of my buddies I knew that I would be loading back up on the Stryker tomorrow and be right back out on another patrol. For me, I could easily tell Caz to stay behind but I hated missing the opportunity to head out and possibly miss any chance to get some action. Besides, if something happened to my buddies and I wasn't there then I would feel responsible and that feels worse than any damage an IED could do.

CHAPTER 7
Friday the 13th

13 October 2006, Friday the 13th and we are set up inside the Iraqi Police compound right now. It's been a quiet morning for us and we stopped by a new checkpoint on Route Sword to check out the building progress. This new checkpoint has started to cause a lot of problems for Insurgents which in turn causes a lot of problems for us. They don't want it there so they continuously attack it and try to destroy it making it difficult for any Iraqi Police or Army officials to occupy. This morning, thankfully, it was still there.

I am starting to get a little bored with the Police visits, it seems all we do is sit there and wait for anything to go wrong. The Police officials are feeding us lies to cover up any crooked deals going on in their organization and the only two things I really like about coming here is the Chai (Tea) and a little black dog that we have named, Jihad. He is just a little stray dog that we have been bringing food for and he loves sitting on the back ramp of the Stryker and letting us pet him. We keep our gloves on because there is a lot of disease in this neighborhood and often wash up as soon as we are done playing.

Another thing I don't like about coming here is the fact that we have to drive right past where my Stryker was blown up not too long ago. I am not really scared that it will happen again it's just frustrating to think that whoever set off the attack got away with it. I have been searching the Internet for propaganda videos of the attack but since no one was killed it will probably not be posted. I am still pissed off over the whole thing and haven't been able to lift weights since the incident. I did manage to lift over 295 pounds before I got hurt, though.

I am starting to see just how much politics is playing a role in this war. Iraqis fighting other types of Iraqis trying to gain territory while we are stuck in the middle bouncing back and forth between them and they don't want us there because it's not our fight but we still try. There is so much bullcrap going on that its difficult for any of us to stop and think about what exactly we are doing here. Take the dog, Jihad, for instance; he is completely innocent and all he wants is a little attention and food. We come to his aid and give him these necessities but along comes a terrorist, kills the dog and stuffs an IED in him to use against us and all we did was try to help. Where is the solution in that?

But as frustrated as we get over this whole thing we are still here and we still have to look out for each other. We look to each other for protection and when we are in the crap, we do whatever it takes to keep our brothers alive, even if it means taking the life of an innocent bystander. This is a big reason why we are getting such a bad name for ourselves back in the states. Because our Government is pressing a life of Democracy on a Country that bases its life on Religion and nothing can change that. So we are here to force it on them but in the end we are losing our lives over something that will probably never change and even if it does it will most likely be a temporary fix. I guess the world will see and I hope I am proven wrong.

15 October 2006, holy crap all this bitching and complaining has finally paid off We are finally moving into a better area into little metal buildings with air conditioning and real beds It's like Christmas here and SGT Reider and I have gotten a lucky break by getting one of the larger rooms. We have been scouring the area for TVs, a refrigerator, a stereo, and anything else that we can use to make our little shack feel like civilization. Reider and I have a decent collection of DVD movies and CDs and often make trips to the local Hajji shop to by pirated movies for a pretty low price.

In these shops you can find just about anything from Iraqi energy drinks called Wild Tigers, which has become a new addiction for me, complete sets of popular TV shows like The A-Team or even Highlander but that's a different story for a different day.

It is amazing how the simplest things we get here make it so much easier for us to tolerate the crap we go through. After a long mission it's nice to just crack open a cold soda in the chow hall. So many people take things like that for granted and don't really know how to appreciate their lives any more. I could spend a day searching for dead bodies or patrolling through dangerous neighborhoods and come back to the FOB, drag my feet all the way back to my cool little room and sit down in front of the TV and just feel completely perfect. If I could share one thing with the world at these moments it is this; never give up a chance to enjoy a nice sunset, never pass up a hug from a loved one, never walk away from a cool juicy piece of fruit and never take the little things in life for granted. Because, someday all these things will be gone and you won't be able to get them back.

This Friday the 13th I was feeling a little extra crazy and decided to start writing to get a kind of release from feeling that way....so I wrote a little poem to amuse my buddies:

A Poor Excuse for a Song

Picture this if you will,
A happy couple named Lois and Phil,
With two good children named Bobby and Jill
Who, when walking from school were shot and killed.

Little Bobby was hit in the head,
But Jill took two in the heart instead,
Gasping for life as they both still bled,
Then seconds later, both of them were dead.

It wasn't a robbery, it wasn't a gang.
A bully was picking on Jill when the bell rang,
And Bobby tried to help he cried and he sang,
Leave her alone Ill blow out your brains!

It was only a threat, he had no gun
He grabbed his sister and started to run.
They started to walk, when they knew they were done
They saw a quick flash and the bully had won.

Lois and Phil have said their good byes
One million tears for one thousand cries
And weep in their home they try and they try
To dream of a place where nobody dies.
I don't think it will be a Grammy winner but the music is pretty catchy. Besides, who says I will make it back from this crap hole anyway?

CHAPTER 8
The New Checkpoint

16 October 2006, was another bad day. Of course, there really haven't been very many good days, but today 1st Platoon was out over watching the new check point on Route Sword and RPG alley when they got mortared. As they were evacuating the area SSG Kaiser, a former roommate of mine, was in the Squad Leaders hatch of his squads Stryker. He was trying to talk to the driver, giving him directions and as he looked over the side a mortar landed right next to the vehicle. In the attack his eye came out of its socket and had to be evacuated to the Aid Station.

This checkpoint has been the object of a lot of attention and we have asked for it to be leveled several times. No Iraqi personnel will man the checkpoint for fear that it will get attacked so we have to force them to stay there and pull an over watch from a nearby house to make sure they are doing their freaking job. I can't even count with my fingers how many times this place has been attacked either with American or Iraqi personnel and has had to been rebuilt a couple of times already.

Now after this attack, 15 mortars fell on 1st Platoon and SSG Kaiser was being rushed to the FOB for treatment. Kaiser, a taller, skinny guy was transferred from another Company after nearly rolling a Stryker during our last deployment. He moved into the barracks at the same time I was living there and became my roommate for a short period of time. He was always a pretty good guy and always made me laugh and now I was stuck on the FOB waiting to hear a status report on how he was doing.

Every time I know a Platoon is out on a mission or patrol and I am on the FOB I make it a point to check in with the CP to talk to the radio watch just for any information on how everyone is doing. I hate hearing a blast or small arms fire when any one is out because I never know if we are going to have to rush to the motor pool and load up the Stryker to go help out. I still feel responsible for not being out when C32 was hit and I know I am not the only one that feels that way too. But that is the nature of the beast when it comes to being in an Infantry Unit. We can't always be out and we can't always be save the world, that's one thing that makes this job so hard at times and it will always be that way.

17 October 2006, another sleepless night for me.Doc gave me some muscle relaxers to help with the pain in my shoulder and it seems that they are the only things that help me relax any

more. I am almost out but luckily I have been able to find substitutes. I have found that mixing muscle relaxers with a large amount of Tylenol PMs will give quite a buzz. The PMs pack quite a kick and I have been chewing about of them at a time just to help me get to sleep.

I either can't sleep because of the pain or I take so much crap that I pass out and then I have the most ate up dreams and usually wake up from them in a cold sweat. Sometimes I accidentally take too many pills and end up wandering around my room or outside all night and now, on top of everything else, there is a new anti-mortar system on the FOB that fires thousands of 9mm rounds at a time to knock a mortar out of the sky as it falls to the FOB. I don't know if the system works or not but they have been test firing it a lot lately and it is so loud that even if I am sleeping it will scare the living crap out of me. Of course I have been pretty jumpy lately but I think that is because we have had so many mortars landing close to our rooms lately.

I don't always need to take the pills, though, because we will spend up to 2hours outside the wire and when we get back my body just shuts down without the aid of meds. I have spoken to the doc about this and he is recommending that I go see mental health but that won't happen. I am not going to risk getting pulled off the line because I am having some bad dreams and rough nights without sleep. I am sure I will adapt just like I always do, I have to.

CHAPTER 9
Ink and Needles

21 October 2006 The pills weren't working any more, the doc wasn't being a very big help and I was starting to think that I should just accept it and learn to live with all the hate and anger growing in me.

Today, however, I have found my salvation in the form of a little ink and a few needles. My buddy, SSG Mikey Ewing told me that a guy in his section by the name of SSG George Vash is quite the tattoo artist. He said I should just go talk to him and see about getting some tattoo work done and after a little influencing I decided to pay him a visit.

SSG Vash's room was a long way away from my room so I had a long walk and when I finally arrived I smelled something familiar that I hadn't smelled for a long time; green soap Green soap is a liquid used in tattoo shops to clean the skin for tattooing. I have been getting tattoos since I was a Private and it has become almost like an addiction for me. For me, there is just something about a couple hours of getting inked that makes the pain go away. It's almost like trading emotional pain for physical pain and it's a therapy that I have turned to many times before.

SSG George Vash was a quiet and fairly angry guy that most people avoided because he had a tendency to not like people. I was a little nervous to bother him but not scared. He was an average height guy with tattoos all over his arms and a shaved head. At first site you might think he was anti social but really I think he is just picky when it comes to making friends. He was a tanker, like Mikey, and served on the ATGM (Anti-Tank Guided Missile) version of the Stryker. It was getting late and fairly dark but after about 3minutes of walking around I finally found the room.

As I stepped into his room it was almost like walking in to a miniature tattoo shop. There were sketches and tattoo photos all over his walls and he had a decent little set up. I managed to talk him into giving me a tattoo of a drawing that I did years ago of the popular comic character, Johnny the Homicidal Maniac a dark and sinister character hunched over with a large carving knife in his hand.

It started off as any typical tattoo would with the soap and shaving the arm. I decided to put this particular piece on my left fore-arm behind a fire wrist band that I had done before I left. After the shave he laid a carbon copy-like piece of paper on my arm and pealed it up leaving the design on my arm in a blue color outline. I was excited to hear a tattoo gun fire up again, it was already starting to take me away from this place. I was back in one of my favorite places again, the tattoo shop.

He began to lay the outline down and almost as soon as the needles first hit my arm I felt the rush of endorphins flow through me and for the first time in weeks I felt good. He had a heavy hand and I started to bleed right away but I have always been a bleeder and the sight of it was a form of therapy all in its self. I wasn't worried about infection at all because he wore gloves and everything in the room was wiped down with alcohol prior to starting. The needles were brand new out of the package and the gun was sterilized. The only problem would be keeping it clean during missions because we weren't exactly in a clean environment but I didn't care at that point.

By the time he was finished with the outline, Mikey was in there and it was time for a break. We stepped outside for a smoke break and as we were lighting up a couple guys walked by and saw the fresh ink and blood on my arm and instantly started talking about wanting to get tattoos. I looked at SSG Vash and said, Hey did you ever think about making a little money on the side while you are here? He said it was probably a bad idea because he could get in trouble, even though he really didn't care, but he said he would hook up his buddies and everyone else would have to wait until we were home.

We stepped back inside and got started again this time finishing up the shading and filling. After about another hour of bleeding and inking he was finally finished. I was very pleased with how it looked and had Mikey take several pictures. I got to be part of something that very few people could be part of. I got to tell people that I got a tattoo in the middle of a war zone and if I made it back to the states it would be a great conversation story. I think I remember paying Vash about a hundred bucks and it was so late that I was ready to try and get some sleep.

That night I slept better than I have ever slept from taking pills. I laid down on my bed careful to rest my arm where it wouldn't bleed everywhere and the tingling pain in my arm was starting to fill the rest of my body making me feel surprisingly numb to the rest of the world. I quickly closed my eyes and before I knew it I was out. I slept like a baby that night and something inside of me told me that I would be paying Vash a few more visits before we got out of this place.

22 October 2006, today we have just locked horns with the

Battalion Commander, LTC Smiley, that is to say one of our Staff Sergeants did.SSG Staggs, a Squad Leader from 2nd Platoon made world-wide news today when he was interviewed about his opinion of this war.

Before I say too much about SSG Staggs I have to say that I freaking hate the mediate doesn't matter what news team or network they always cut out the important crap and show all the bad crap making us all look bad. This is one of the reasons why there are a large number of people in the United States who protest and hate us and the war. This is exactly what happened to SSG Staggs.

In so many words he stated that this was not our war, meaning that we, The Infantry, have no place in Iraq. The people of Iraq do not want us here and they certainly do not want our democracy leaving us here to fight and die for pretty much no reason at all. Almost as quickly as his interview went someone had already put it on the internet and this caught the eyes of all the Command elements.

I am not sure exactly how our Battalion Commander reacted but I am sure that he was pretty upset, at least that's what I heard.SSG Staggs wasn't fired and didn't get in trouble but he said what he felt was the truth and nearly every soldier in country felt the same way.LTC Smiley probably got his ass chewed for the interview and in turn would have had to say something to SSG Staggs for being honest on world-wide news.

LTC Avanulus Smiley, our Battalion Commander was a larger guy and very outspoken. If something pissed him off he wouldn't hesitate to say something about it. He walked strong and carried a black steal tomahawk, the symbol of our Battalion, The Tomahawks. He came to us with very large shoes to fill, however, and he was doing pretty well.

Last deployment we had LTC Buck James, an even larger man who shaved his head and made it a point in his career to step on as many toes as he could. One would say he was the modern day General Patton and all the veterans in the Battalion always compared LTC Smileys tactics to Buck and this upset LTC Smiley but didn't slow him down one bit. He would often be seen on patrols especially when a fire fight broke out.

As soon as a Company would take any sort of contact we would start to listen to the Battalion Net and would always hear the BC (Battalion Commander) let us know that he was on his way. I have personally witnessed him and the Battalion Sergeant

Major standing in the middle of streets during missions even if we were taking any sort of small-arms fire. Some would say it was stupid but I would have to admit that it took a lot of balls. They did manage to get in our way a few times but who can argue with the Battalion Commander?

I got a chance to speak to SSG Staggs not long after his interview and shook his hand and told him not to be discouraged because it took a lot of guts to say what he said and I only hope that the people of the United States can start to see that they aren't the only ones who hate this war. But no matter what we feel and no matter what our opinion is of this war, we still swore an oath and we will stick by it to the death.

23 October 2006, Ramadan is over and we have been able to catch a bit of the World Series on TV, even though the game would come on very early in the morning so if we weren't on patrol we would sneak up to the CP and watch. I am originally from Missouri and my favorite baseball team is the St. Louis Cardinals. I consider Washington state to be home though and I love the Seattle Seahawks which pisses off a lot of the guys here from Missouri, but the first time I ever saw an NFL game in person it was at Qwest Field and the Seahawks destroyed the Chicago Bears and I have been hooked ever since.

The Cardinals, however were doing okay so far against the Detroit Tigers, they have just lost Game 2 of the Series. I was pretty upset because I stayed up so late to watch the game. I got a box from my mom and my grandparents with some Cardinals gear which I put on as much as I could during the games. I even wore one of the T-shirts under my uniform during missions for good luck.

I didn't feel very lucky today, however, because as we were coming back in the gate from a patrol I got stung on the neck by huge wasp. This was no ordinary wasp that can be seen back in the United States and I actually grabbed it right after it got me and it felt like a large rock. I even smacked it pretty hard and it flew away as if I had just barely tapped it.

I quickly grabbed my digital camera to take a picture of my neck just to see what it looked like and only seconds after getting stung my neck was already swelling up like a balloon. I am a little allergic to bee stings but haven't had any problems since I was a kid but I was starting to get nervous. The doc just told me to put ice on it and I started to have trouble breathing to say something about it. I was more shocked that the wasp was so large, it seems like everything here is bigger, especially the spiders.

I am not scared of spiders at all, but a camel spider will make any man turn around and walk the other way. Luckily, this deployment we really didn't have very many encounters with camel spiders, but last deployment was almost like a non-stop camel spider festival and if you ever saw one in person you would never forget it. They are not poisonous but they are nasty looking and I have seen them get bigger than a man's head. They would climb up the walls of bunkers that we stayed in and fall on us from the ceiling while we laid in our cots. Most of us slept with our sleeping bags completely zipped up over our heads.

One thing I will say about this country is that there is no other place on Earth like it. We could put thousands of Burger Kings and Taco Bells here and it would still be like living in an episode of The Twilight Zone. If I live through this deployment, Iraq and the time I have spent here will always be a large part of me.

CHAPTER 10
A Convoy of Cowards

25 October 2006, Another day and we have to go patrol out to the freaking police station again. The monotony of all this is getting to the point of we could probably execute this mission in our sleep. My Stryker, along with Caz and LT Rogers, was attached to the Tanker section again. The standard preparation applies to every mission; walk to the motor pool, drive the Strykers up to the chow hall parking lot near the ice point. At that point the drivers and dismounts would either get chow or assist in filling coolers with ice and bottles of water or Gatorade. After we had accountability of everyone we mounted up, gave the ready status (Redcon One) and rolled out towards the gate.

The gate guards hated us because every time we passed by them we would give them crap. You better have chow waiting when we get back! we would shout through our loud speakers and then soon after crank up some AC/DC or any loud music to motivate us as we drove up Thunder Run which is the route that takes us from the gate to the MSR. Once we got to the MSR we would shut off the music and it was pretty much Game On from that point.

Traveling to the IP station was simple and difficult at the same time. Constantly scanning the roads for possible IEDs or EFPs, we were always alert. The rear air guards would scan roof tops, windows of nearby buildings, and cars that would weave in and out of our convoy. Any time the cars would get close we would point a laser sight at them or fire a couple paint ball rounds at them to get them to back off. We had a lot of non-lethal weapons for those purposes.

Once we made it to the IP station we would quickly set up a small security area as each Stryker would back into the small compound one at a time. We were pretty much covered by a large brick wall, however, some of the dismounts would climb to the roof and pull security while key leaders would enter the IP station and begin talking to the Police Chief or whoever was in charge that day. Depending on who was there we would either get a lot of information on dirty cops, possible terrorist activity in the neighborhood, and other things but much of the time we would leave empty handed and the IPs were getting quite sick of us bothering all the time.

I made it a point to get out of the Stryker every once in a while to get some chain or bread, but most of the time I would just assume Battle Position 1 which is the code name I gave for the troop bench for a quick nap. Caz had the best seat in the

Stryker because the driver's seat has the potential to lay back completely however the temperature up there can get quite hot in the middle of the Iraqi summer.

Today was a different mission all together because we were to pick up a few of the Iraqi Police and drive them out to one of the smaller FOBs near FOB Liberty for a little public relations. We have found that the more we interact with the Iraqis the more they feel like we want to be equals even though most of the time they won't let us. We don't always visit for questioning, sometimes we will come just to play football or in this case, take them to a range and let them shoot American rifles.

We pulled in to the little Outpost and immediately staged the Strykers in a parking area. On this Outpost there is a tiny man made range for shooting smaller weapons or personal rifles. We gathered the IPs at the firing line and began to give them some instruction on our American M4 Carbines and they in turn were giving us instruction on their AK-47s even though most of us already knew how to use them.

No sooner did we get to show them how to load our rifles did we hear a large amount of gun fire coming from the direction of Route Sword almost directly to the North.LT Rogers asked me to begin monitoring the NET because our 1st Platoon was out on a routine patrol in that area.

Right away we began to hear 1st PLT on the NET reporting contact on Route Sword and needed assistance in securing a convoy. We knew that it would take some time for QRF (Quick Reaction Force) to mount up and get to them so we quickly mounted up along with the IPs and headed towards the direction of the shooting.

We came off of the overpass on to Route Sword just East of Race Track road and we immediately saw our 1st Platoon Strykers trying to secure a military convoy carrying M1 Abrahm Tanks. A Platoon of Strykers is only four vehicles and this convoy was much too large for them to secure.

The convoy was traveling East on Route Sword to deliver the tanks to another unit when they were ambushed from nearby houses and alleys. Our section began to peel off around the convoy towards the front of them. My vehicle was at the immediate tip of the convoy pulling security down a 40meter stretch of highway beginning to clutter up with traffic and people.

We immediately began to assess the situation and since we

had Tankers with us they decided to try and dismount under enemy fire to download the tanks off of the flat bed trucks because they had caught fire from enemy rounds. Our section NCOIC (Non Commissioned Officer in Charge), SFC Palma, met up with the convoy commander on the ground as they were being attacked. They used a nearby vehicle as cover to discuss and assess the situation and all SFC Palma could understand that the Convoy Commander was freaking out and locking up under the stress of being ambushed. He had no idea what to do and none of the drivers in the convoy knew how to operate the tanks they were carrying.

SFC Palma, LT Rogers, and our 1st Platoon Leader decided we should take matters into our own hands and immediately began to secure the tanks. We were still under fire and as I was scanning we began to hear mortar rounds impacting nearby us. A section from another Company arrived and a soldier from that section dismounted to assist our guys when he was hit by a round in his lower back putting him on the ground. Our guys secured the soldier and got him onto a Stryker to be treated.

At this point we looked at some of the soldiers that were part of the convoy hiding in their armored trucks and some of them didn't even have body armor on. This is a product of getting lazy and complacent and it was no surprise for us to see this due to the lack of discipline their own Convoy Commander had under pressure. Then, they did something that none of us expected; they disconnected the trailers with the tanks still on them and began to move out.

We watched in shock as they moved away from us and the enemy fire began to pick up. Not only did they leave the millions of dollars worth of M1 tanks, but they also took their trucks away leaving our guys on the ground completely exposed as they climbed on to the tanks to start them up.

Caz began to yell at me in the head set that we were taking fire from a window off to our right immediately scanned over to the window and could make out the figure of a man and then spotted muzzle flash coming from there. I didn't hesitate to put my cross hairs on the center of the window and squeezed the trigger. It was almost like watching a slow motion movie as I saw my rounds tear into the brick wall around the window and then I saw a large splash of red explode through the window and could see the headless body of the man fall to the floor inside the building. I felt a rush of adrenaline unlike I have never felt before and I immediately had a large smile of my face as I told Caz that I had just got my first kill of the deployment. He was just as happy because he helped me spot the guy. I immediately reported the kill on the Company Net just to cover my own ass in case we had to do a report if we made it back.

SPC Rosario, a Tanker still mounted on his Stryker reported that he had been hit in his hand and I had Caz pull the Stryker back to cover Rosario's vehicle and that's when I noticed the guys on the ground were taking fire from a building only about 5meters away from them. Myself and another Stryker opened up with our Machine Guns and ripped the house to pieces stopping the enemy fire immediately.

By this time the Tanks were nearly downloaded and the mortar fire began to increase with the rounds impacting closer and closer to our position. This could only mean that there was a Hajj with eyes on us and was talking to the mortar man walking the rounds on to us. A soldier from 1st Platoon spotted a man watching us from his car and talking on his cell phone as this was happening. Considering that this man was so close to an ambush site while we were under fire and instead of fleeing the scene he was on the phone more than likely a bad guy so the soldier opened fire on the man with his M4 killing him instantly and ending the mortar fire almost immediately. It was a risky move but worth it to make is a little safer for us to finish what we were doing.

We got word from our guys on the ground that the Tanks were ready to move and we all got back into a vehicle formation and headed back to the FOB.I looked up out of my hatch to take a few pictures of the convoy with my digital camera and I could see my buddy Vash and his guys along with Mikey and the rest of the Tankers driving these beasts back to the FOB with huge grins on their faces.

Our Tankers don't drive Tanks instead they have a variation of the Stryker known as the ATGM (Anti-Tank Guided Missile) that fires a missile off the top instead of a large cannon like they are used torso this mission was a success in many ways because we secured millions of dollars worth of equipment, my buddies got to drive tanks again, and I got my first kill of the tour

As we pulled back on to the FOB we gave the Gate Guards more crap, Hey were back, where my chow?!Did you miss us?!They watched in awe as we pulled our Strykers and new

Tanks through the gate and we could tell they were jealous. The most action they see is a couple pop shots from the field across the road.

We parked back at the chow hall parking lot and began to dismount to assess any damage on our vehicles. Caz spotted a couple places around his drivers hatch that had been hit by enemy fire and the whole right side of our Stryker had tiny pieces of armor chipped away by small arms. I didn't care, because we were all still alive and I was still feeling the rush of watching a man's head explode. I spotted my old squad leader, SSG Casarez, in the parking lot and the first thing that came out of my mouth was, I killed a guy! I was excited and couldn't wait to park the Stryker so I could go back to the tent and brag to the guys who had to stay in the rear.

About an hour later I was sitting on my cot with some of my gear still on just thinking to myself about all that had happened today. It was a shock to think that I had survived a pretty heavy attack, and took a man's life in the process. I could still see it happen over and over every time I closed my eyes and even though I was excited I started to question what I had done. I wondered if the man had kids, of if he was still a kid himself. I wondered if it was just a guy standing in a window and if what I thought might be muzzle flash could have been him lighting a cigarette. But I caught myself questioning the whole thing and immediately pushed it to the back of my mind because I had to make room just in case I had more figures to store. We weren't even half way through this deployment and I didn't want to risk having any sympathetic feelings for the morons that had gotten us here in the first place.

We later found out that the same convoy that tucked tail and ran away from an attack had gotten ambushed again farther down the road and ended up leaving another truck containing the uniform top of an American soldier. This sparked a whole mess of us getting geared up to go look for a possibly missing soldier until we found out that the kid had been riding around without his top. It amazes me just how relaxed some of the units are around here. This one mistake could have put us at risk for another attack and every time we roll out we have the potential of getting hurt or killed. I only hope that it was a lesson learned for this unit although I doubt it will have any effect on them what-so-ever.

CHAPTER 11
The Verdict

5 November 2006, it has been a couple weeks since our big Tank rescue and it is already a distant memory. The Command wants to give us all awards for the mission but I really don't see the need for me to get anything because I was doing what I was trained to do. I was just doing my job, the same as I have been doing since I got here, fire fight or not. I think that the only guys that should get any sort of recognition were the guys that were on the ground recovering the equipment under fire. They risked their lives to assist another unit and to secure sensitive Army equipment and, to me, that sounds like award material but we will see what happens.

Today was to be a historic and memorable day for everyone involved. We were back at the Iraqi Police station again for a typical patrol when we were told that Sadaam Hussein had finally been sentenced to death for the crimes he committed when he was in power. We were excited to hear the news but at the same time we had to be ready for anything. As soon as we were told of the news we could hear a lot of AK-47 fire opening up all around us in the city and we mounted up ready for any attacks or riots that may occur.

Most of the gun fire was celebratory and we all watched outside the gate of the IP compound as Iraqi car after Iraqi car was racing around the neighborhood with lots of people standing on top of them, singing songs and waving flags out of excitement that the man that had been oppressing them was finally going to pay for his actions. It was a very inspirational sight to watch people come together and I am sure it there was a lot of closure for them. We were ordered to be on our guard but to let them celebrate without interruption. I was ready for anything but managed to take a few good pictures of the historic event that was happening right in front of our eyes.

It was during our last deployment that we were told Hussein had been captured by elements from 101st Airborne. It was at the very beginning of our tour and we were staged to roll out from a place called FOB Pacesetter. This FOB was where a lot of Units prepared their vehicles and equipment before rolling out and starting their tours. It was cold, wet, muddy and we were just waiting around to get the word to move out when our Company Commander, then CPT Fred Tanner, told us the news. I remember his words well, Men, Sadaam Hussein has been captured The war is NOT over The enemy is amassing on us as we speak! There was a moment of excitement that he had finally been captured but it was quickly interrupted when we were told to pack up our stuff because we were, going into the Lion's Den!

Now, years later, he was finally sentenced to be hanged and we finally had mixed feelings of relief and some doubt. It was hard to believe that it was all happening and we knew that even after he was to be hanged it would really make no difference in the pace of the war. Other leaders would follow in his footsteps and we could catch every one of them only to be replaced by another. It was a vicious cycle and it seemed like there would always be this terror all around no matter what religion these people followed. Don't get me wrong, I didn't care who they were or what they believed, if they shot at me I would shoot back without hesitation, but it almost seemed pointless to keep our hopes up that this would end in any sort of peace. But peace didn't seem to be in the schedule and this only reconfirmed our opinions in that we would keep fighting to keep each other alive and let the politicians deal with the rest of the bull crap.

7 November 2006, business as usual and it has been two days since the verdict of Sadaam Hussein and we have just received word that Alpha Company took a bad hit in their area of operations yesterday. They were traveling on Ghazalia Main, the route that runs past the IP station, when they were hit by multiple EFPs. The bomb hit their Stryker seriously wounding three soldiers and killing one named SGT White.

I did not know him very well, but if you spend enough time in a Unit you start to get to know soldiers from other Companies in the Battalion. I remember SGT White being a pretty funny guy from seeing him outside our Battalion area back on Fort Lewis. Although our Company didn't really know him we will most likely be invited to the Memorial held here on FOB Liberty in the small Chapel near our CP.

Once again, we are put in a position to question whether or not we should be here. I am constantly finding myself lying in my bed all night trying to justify reasons why we had to come here and I know I am not the only one who is asking these questions. But I nor anyone else here have the right or rank to ask questions like that so we drive on through the political bull crap and continue fighting. This too shall pass a popular quote around here and also something I say to myself on a daily basis. It helps me get through times like this.

66

Still, it is a sad time for our brothers in Alpha Company and we have to be strong for them, SGT Whites family, and also the other soldiers wounded in the attack.

I am trying to keep my head straight because CPT Pike will be leaving us soon and we will be receiving a new Company Commander. This is typical in any Army Unit to see Commanders come and go and I will miss working with him but I am sure we will see each other sometime down the road. I am also going on mid-tour leave soon and I have decided to go back to Missouri and spend the time with my family from my home town area. I don't even know if I want to leave because I don't want anything to happen to anyone while I am away. I am sure I will be glued to the television and internet looking for any news on my buddies here just to know they are safe. But no matter how much time I spend back in the States I know I will never really be leaving this place.

12 November 2006, today was the day of SGT Whites memorial service and walking around I could feel a heavy weight on everyone in our Battalion. I couldn't make it to the service but I remember hearing the 21 Gun Salute and Taps being played so I stopped what I was doing for a moment to think about the situation.

It's hard to notice that there is a memorial service going on when it is happening just by looking at the rest of the soldiers on this FOB. They are all running around in their PT uniforms, relaxed because it wasn't their unit that got hit; it wasn't their buddy that was killed. I don't expect them to all stop what they are doing just because we lose a guy, but it's almost as if they are all on vacation, collecting that big pay check every two weeks just to dodge a few mortars every now and then. I know they all have purposes, for the most part, but are we the only ones doing all the fighting? Once again I have to remind myself, This too shall pass.

CHAPTER 12
Hurry Up and Wait

15 November 2006, I realize that it takes a special type of person to do what we do for a living. We risk our lives on a daily basis, fighting against enemies both seen and unseen, spending months in a country where we are completely hated and that calls for a certain type of mentality in a man. What I mean by all this is; you have to be a little messed up in the head to put up with what we do on any given day in the Infantry The last couple of nights have been a complete test on our mental strength on many levels.

The night before last we were put on standby because Platoons from Alpha Company and Bravo Company were attacked with multiple IEDs, RPGs (Rocket Propelled Grenades).We were all on stand-by for hours waiting to go assist the units in any way we could however as I stood in the CP and watched the map on the big screen we could clearly see that there was no way to get to them.

The area they were being attacked was north of our sector across a small bridge and up a narrow road that paralleled the creek. It was a text book ambush and the more vehicles that went in the more blocked in they could get. We listened for a good few hours and the tension was building more and more as we listened to the frantic radio chatter.

We were all here ready to go and support but there was no way to get to them so we were helpless. There were already Strykers damaged and disabled that would have to be recovered not to mention wounded troops that would have to be evacuated as soon as possible and all of this at night. It was hard for us to tell just how many enemy personnel there were but we knew it wasn't good. We only had a couple options; either move North and cover their movement back to the FOB, take over their position if they were able to get themselves out, or just sit on the FOB and hope that they all made it out alive.

We were finally told to stand down and the units up North would self-recover the disabled Strykers and moved back. I remember being frustrated that we had been on standby for so long and sitting helplessly the entire night, but I was glad that someone had finally made a decision. I never got the full details of the attack on the units but I know that one Stryker burned to the ground. I walked back to the chow hall parking lot, where we were staged, and told my crew to stand down.

As we were powering down the Stryker we got word to prepare for raids to be conducted on a Mosque and another building. We began to set out the gear we needed and once again we were on stand-by. For the next several hours into the early morning we were told to move out about 6 or 7 times and ended being stopped every time. We were all lying around the Strykers with our gear next to us. When we would get the word to move out we would grab our kits and put them on, then in about 3seconds we would all be loaded on to the Strykers with the ramps up.

We would send the word up to the Battalion CP that we were REDCON 1 and they would in turn tell us to stand by. About 5 or 1minutes later they would tell us to stand down until eventually the whole mission was called off. We spent most of the night running around the parking lot throwing a football around, joking with each other, smoking cigarettes, and just acting like complete fools. We never expected to go since the raid was to be on a Mosque.

We knew in the back of our minds that it would be too much of a liability to risk damaging a Mosque and at this point of the war we are trying to win the hearts and minds of the local people, which is a joke to most of us. We have already been limited in so many ways on what we can and cannot do here. We can't fire MK-19s or our TOW missiles because we can't make a big mess. The Stryker that burned down from the attack last night caused a little damage and the Battalion was already printing apology letters to the people around there because of the damage we caused by getting ambushed.

Any time we know where insurgent lives and we go kick his door down to capture him, we have to pay for the door and send our best apologies to the family of the insurgent for damaging their property. If we get attacked and fire back we have to pay for anything we damage in the process. I understand if we accidentally kick down a door and it turns out to be the wrong house or we got bad information, then we can pay for the door. But, we put our lives at risk when we are entering these houses and we always take a chance of being shot as soon as we enter the door. To me that is payment enough for catching these morons and making the world a safer place.

17 November 2006, part of being in this war is the potential for showing new Units around by giving them a few rides in the Strykers. Today we took out a Brigade Commander from another Unit for a little look around our area of operations. Everything

started off normal, we got him in the rear hatch of my Stryker and we gave him a helmet with a microphone so that we could talk back and forth during the trip.

We went to the West end of our sector and then up north passing by a couple bodies along the way that had been there for a few days already. After reporting the bodies we moved east to Ghazalia Main and then back down to the South to Route Sword and as we were making our way down the ramp on to the MSR we heard a loud Pop! sound and as I looked to the right I saw an RPG coming straight for us I could see it speeding with a loud hissing sound and only about 5meters away from my Stryker it is a small power line on the side of the ramp detonating it instantly.

We were attached to 1st Platoon at the time and I could hear one of my buddies over the NET announce that he spotted enemy on a building and was going to engage. Every Stryker with a machine gun on it quickly traversed on to the building and I quickly jumped down to my gunners station and began to engage with my gun also!

I watched in my Fire Control Unit as we all lit up the same building and anything in or around it could not have survived It was like watching a war movie unfold right in front of mammy Commander and the Brigade Commander in the rear hatch began to fire with their rifles also We kept the rate of fire up for a good 2to 3seconds, still moving down the ramp towards the highway. It seemed like it lasted for about an hour and before we knew it we were entering the highway. I scanned the area that we had fired at and saw a much damaged building but no sign of enemy kills.

We made the decision to head back and as we were rolling towards the FOB the Brigade Commander made it a point to thank me several times and couldn't believe that we had almost been hit by an RPG.I assured him that the Stryker could take an RPG hit and the chances of the rocket actually penetrating the armor was small but possible. He was still thankful and we all felt pretty lucky. I am pretty sure that I will be able to remember that RPG coming right at me for the rest of my life, along with everything else I have seen here. We live to fight another day.

For the rest of the day we were on standby so I got to chill out in my room and try to get some sleep. Sleep has been becoming more and more scarce lately. I find myself taking more and more pills just to get my eyes shut. I don't want to go but I think I will have to go back to the Aid Station and talk to the Doc about this. I know I am not completely crazy, but I need to get some sleep. I doubt that my body can handle too much more of this.

22 November 2006, I had some downtime today so I went to visit with one of our Company medics to ask him some questions. I am a bit embarrassed to go to the Aid Station and talk about my feelings with the Major in charge. I haven't slept for a few days and even though I am tired I can't seem to relax enough. The mortar rounds have been landing closer and closer to the area where we all sleep and I can't seem to shut my eyes without thinking about the fact that a round might land on top of my room and I won't wake up the next morning.

Our Company medics are pretty cool, they seem to know what they are doing, which is a great thing in our line of work, but it's tough for someone who has been nothing but a soldier for the last several years to admit that he is having problems. But, I know that if I don't get any sleep soon that it will probably start to affect my ability to perform on missions. I don't want anything to happen to Caz if I fail to do my job with 100% performance.

Caz doesn't seem to be affected at all by anything that goes on here. He just smiles and does what I ask without question and he always cheers me up when I get pissed off. I couldn't imagine going through this with any other driver, except maybe for Specialist Doranski, my alternate driver.

I finally got to our medics room and told him everything going on and he ended up walking with me to the Aid Station to see the PA (physician's assistant). I sat there for about an hour before he gave me some pills to help me sleep for the next few days and he also recommended that I keep a sleep journal based on nights that I take the pill, if I have a nightmare to write it down, if I can't sleep at all write it down. He also said to add my sleep and hygiene habits.

He said that I should try to get to sleep the same time every night, which is impossible since we are out at different times every day, but I was going to try my best to follow the rules; it couldn't hurt. I didn't really care, I needed to sleep or I could be putting myself and others at risk.

As far as work goes, its business as usual.3rd Platoons

Platoon Sergeant and Platoon Leader were relieved due to personal differences. Our 4th Platoon also has new leadership named LT Morton who came to us from Bravo Company. He's a burly guy who always likes to talk crap to anyone who gets in his way.LT Rogers has moved up to become our Company XO (Executive Officer).

I have to admit that even though LT Rogers and I didn't really get along in the beginning he kind of grew on me, especially since we were blown up together. Every time he sees me he calls me Apes instead of Apel and it annoys the crap out of me but it's kind of funny. We will always be Bash Brothers even though he is a senior officer, and I'm sure that we will keep bumping into each other outside of this war.

I have made several visits to my buddy, Georges, room for more tattoos I am up to 14 tattoos now. hats the thing about me is that I have an addictive personality and I love tattoos. I keep bugging him about starting up this tattoo shop and we have begun to nick name his room, Baghdad Ink after a popular television show, Miami Ink. Between the tattoos and the pills I may actually have a fighting chance at getting some sleep here.

CHAPTER 13
Smoke Em

26 November 2006, there is really not much of a better feeling than to be sitting less than 10meters away from a group of insurgents standing around and they have no idea that you are there. Tonight we received intelligence that there were some hostages being held off or Route Sword near an IA (Iraqi Army) checkpoint and we were ordered to go investigate. We never take hostage situations lightly and we know that every second we waste is a possibility that the hostages will be moved to another location or possible executed.

In Iraq if you are captured by a group of insurgents you are taken to a secret location, usually tortured for long periods of time and then executed. Here you can be captured not for just being an American Soldier, but also for being a certain race, your religious preference, and even if you are caught aiding the Americans in any way. We have found these torture chambers and execution sites before and they are usually a tiled or concrete room with several drains in the floor since torture sessions tend to get pretty bloody.

If you are an American or you are working with Americans then the insurgents will post a video on the internet warning anyone and everyone who aids the American Soldiers that you will be punished for your crimes and shortly after that you are executed usually with a gunshot to the back of the head or beheading.

Tonight we didn't have much intelligence other than we knew there were hostages and we had to investigate the area. We arrived at the scene and began searching through dark buildings and alley ways leaving the Strykers to pull security around the sector and down Route Sword. At night we have thermal cameras on our weapons systems that help us see anything moving around that puts off heat which gives us a huge advantage in locating and destroying enemy troops, positions, and vehicles.

About an hour and a half into the search, LT Morton reported seeing a man taking a pass in the field across the street.CPT Pike said, Roger keep an eye on him. I scanned to where LT Morton was watching and saw the man and then another man coming around the back of a house not even 10meters away. The two men had no idea we were there even though our engines were running. I kept an eye on him until another man came out of the back of the house with what clearly appeared to be a weapon.

LT Morton reported seeing the man with the weapon and as we scanned the house we could see that there was definitely some sort of a meeting going on because we could see several military aged males in the windows and walking around the outside having a quick cigarette break.

Suddenly, two of the men spotted us and began to maneuver to cover and no sooner was it seen that CPT Pike said something I will never forget; Smoke em The men raised their weapons to engage us and we lit up the entire area around the building with our machine guns chopping down some bushes that the men were trying to hide behind.

For the next three to five minutes there was exchange of gun fire from both sides of the roads and we began to observe men beginning to jump from roof top to roof top It was almost like something out of a video game, I have never seen anything like it CPT Pike was firing with his M4 and I watched through my thermal site as he got at least one of those bastards

The firing slowly subsided and the dust began to settle across the road and we saw some hot spots in the grass from the blood of whoever we had shot and after investigating we found that they had quickly evacuated any of their casualties and dead so we had nothing to show for it but some puddles of blood. As for the men that were jumping across the roof tops we don't know where they went and since we already had men on the ground looking for hostages we didn't have any dismounts to go looking.

It was nice to be able to get some trigger time because we have been running ourselves ragged and I needed the adrenaline rush. We all laughed about it when we got back to the FOB but were all pretty tired so we just put the Strykers back in the motor pool and got some rest. It will always amaze me how close we were to those guys the whole time and they didn't spot us until the moment we locked horns and CPT Pikes memorable line, Smoke em quickly became the motto for our Stryker Crew.

CHAPTER 14
The Farmhouse

28 November 2006, every now and then we have to move west of the main city and get into the farm land areas of our AO (Area of Operations).The farm land is a lot of twisting and turning roads with a lot of creeks and deep ditches that make it difficult for us to maneuver our large Strykers through. Last deployment we had an incident where one Stryker rolled off the side of a road and flipped upside down in a creek trapping Squad Members and the crew inside under water. Ever since that day we have had strict policy on how we maneuver around these areas but luckily the area we were going today wasn't like that.

We settled about 200meters west of the city inside the fence of a small farm house. I was facing east and as we searched the area a couple of our Strykers got stuck in some mud so while we waited for them to be self recovered we set up a perimeter around the house.CPT Pike, along with the Company Sniper Team, moved up to the roof of the house and my Stryker sat at the base of the house to cover the edge of the city and one tall Mosque Tower.

In my Stryker I had Caz, of course, and my buddy George and another SGT named Glasscock (you can imagine the nicknames he had).SGT Glasscock, a hick-like individual but a good guy, was out of the rear air guard hatch and George was in the other manning the M24machine gun. We all liked to take these opportunities to eat an MRE (Meal Ready to Eat) and joke around while we scanned our sectors of fire. It was hot and everyone was waiting for the Strykers to get unstuck, when I spotted something in the distance.

In the minute of the Mosque Tower I spotted a dark figure so I decided to investigate with my RWS.As I zoomed on to the object it began to take the shape of a man, which was not out of the ordinary but I decided to get closer. I zoomed in to the full power of my sight and could clearly see a military aged male in the tower with what appeared to be a rifle. I decided to report it to CPT Pike and our Company Sniper SSG Milligan.

Comanche 6this is Comanche 66T, over I called on the Company NET to the roof top above me.66T this is Comanche 69, send it they replied. Roger, check out the mosque tower, does that dude have a rifle? I waited as they investigated. It was common for the Stryker Vehicle Commanders to spot suspicious activity at long ranges but we always reported it unless it was posing an immediate threat. About a minute passed and I decided to call them back but just before I pushed the button to call I heard a shot from the roof top and I quickly scanned to tower observing a round impacting on the side of the tower.

As soon as the Snipers opened up we started taking fire from somewhere along the edge of the city surrounding the mosque tower and we began to return fire For the next few minutes it was a non-stop barrage of suppressive fire along the city line. I could see no enemy personnel outside of the buildings so they were all firing from windows so I switched to thermal sights to try and spot muzzle flashes. I spotted flashes from a few windows near the mosque towers and concentrated my fire on that area.

Glasscock and George began firing with their weapons and then I heard a bang louder than any of our M4s could produce and Glasscock shouted from the back hatch, Don't shoot that freaking thing next to me! George had picked up the .5caliber Sniper Rifle that our Snipers left staged on my Stryker and shoulder fired it with the barrel close to Glasscock's head George started laughing with that sinister chuckle he always got when he was raising hell. I laughed with him until I saw the Low Ammunition warning on my FCU and knew that I was about to climb out of my Stryker to reload my gun under fire.

All Comanche elements this is, Comanche 66T! I called on the NET, I am reloading, cover menthe amount of firing picked up immediately and Glasscock and George stopped firing as I climbed out of my hatch to grab another can of ammunition As soon as I got on top of the Stryker I could hear the rounds of enemy fire snap by my head impacting on the house behind me. I crouched behind the large RWS as I pulled a 10round belt of ammunition from its can and quickly through it into the ammo box feeding it into the .5caliber machine gun My heart was racing as I quickly dove back into the Stryker and called out on the Company NET to announce I was up and began firing again.

CPT Pike called out that he saw fire coming from the tall grass in the field between us and the city edge so I began scanning with my thermal to spot where it was coming from. I saw quite a few cows and sheep and it took me several minutes to spot a heat signature that closely resembled a human and began to lay down fire on that spot. The dismounts spotted where my rounds were landing and began to shoot in the same area. The firing stayed pretty strong for the next 2minutes before the Commander called Cease Fire!

The firing stopped and everyone began scanning with

nothing to report and the enemy in the mosque tower was not visible but I could see a heat signature of what appeared to be fresh blood around the edge of the window.CPT Pike called 1st Platoon to sweep from the South through the buildings we opened fire on. By the time they had gotten there and began investigating they reported no bodies but got a lot of pictures of the damage we did. I thought to myself that we would probably be knocking on doors to pay for damage tomorrow but didn't care. We knew what we were shooting at and we knew that we were getting shot at in return. I double checked myself by looking at the house behind me to make sure that I wasn't dreaming and saw the holes in the walls of the house behind us.

As the Platoon was investigating we began to recover the stuck Strykers again and slowly began to prep for moving out. As we were getting ready we heard a boom from a large IED north-east of our position and heard Battalion report that an element from Bravo Company had been hit and a soldier named SGT Strong had lost his legs and is Platoon Leader had suffered a severe abdominal wound. We also heard a report from Battalion that a local informant called in to the tip-line that there were several planned attacks to be made on American Units today however were disrupted by our Company during the fire fight we had just been through. As unfortunate as the situation for Bravo Company was we knew that we had done the right thing and that we had disrupted enemy activities and we felt a little better, but our hearts and prayers went out for SGT Strong and his Platoon Leader.

3November 2006, last night was interesting, we were pulling an over watch on RPG alleys east and west with the tanker section when they spotted two military aged males getting out of a car with AK-47s and immediately called it up. We were looking for suspected bomb makers and a meeting that was to be going on in the area by known insurgents. Our Battalion Commander cleared them to fire TOW (Tubular launched optically tracked Wire-guided) missile if we spotted them coming back out and trying to leave before we could get a platoon in the house. This made George and Mikey very happy because they hadn't fired a single TOW missile yet But as excited as they were to fire we spotted our 1st Platoon moving on to the house and setting an explosive breach on the door. They had to move in fast because there could be a lot of bad guys in the house and needed to catch them by surprise.

They blew the breach and we watched them quickly enter the house They reported having to detain a man down because he was running for a weapon as they entered the house with non-lethal rounds. Another man didn't resist but a third male went for one of our Squad Leaders rifle so they took him to the ground with force. They searched the house and cars outside finding what appeared to be bomb making material so they took samples and that was enough to detain the men and we loaded them up in the Strykers moving them back to the Detainee Holding Area on our FOB.

The night ended late and we were all pretty tired but we had gotten some good news that a buddy of one of our Platoon Leaders was patrolling through the area west of the city where we were fighting the other day. He said that they found a body in the field, with weapons, and the body was missing an arm and was full of holes made by our machine guns and rifles. I was pretty excited because it confirmed that we were not shooting at ghosts and we got some bragging rights with the rest of the company who made fun of us for all the damage we did that day. His buddy also said that they had found some bomb making material in the buildings we were shooting at so we not only killed an enemy but we stopped them from being able to make and use IEDs or EFPs on American and Iraqi forces. So all in all the day ended on a good note and none of it was in vain.

CHAPTER 15
FOB Life

5 December 2006, we haven't seen much action the last couple days but have had some down time due to the fact that we were going through a Change of Command.CPT Pike was moving up and we were getting a new Commander by the name of CPT Torres. We knew it was coming but dreaded it because with a Change of Command comes a lot of monotonous work. We had to lay out all the Company supply convexes, all our weapons and sensitive items, all the Strykers had to be cleaned and all the equipment had to be laid out. Over the next several days we would layout all of our crap and it would be inspected and inventoried over and over again to account for all of it before the new Commander could go through and sign for all of it.

During this process we have had a chance to get around the FOB and check out some of the stores and get a little fatter eating at Burger King and Taco Bell. The PX, as usual, didn't have anything we wanted because all the FOBBITS had bought it all up, but Reider and I had some time to watch our favorite episodes of Scrubs and the Highlander series. I also took this time to go through some of the pictures and videos I had collected over the last few months and decided that I would make a few movies on my computer to use in a video year book. I was known as the Company media guy and was often used to put together slide shows for the Battalion Commanders meetings he randomly held to keep everyone informed of what had been going on in the Battalion.

The Tattoo Shop was doing great business and had several guys coming in and out for tattoos and George, Mikey and I had set up a nice little place to make some money to be used for a Company Party at the end of the deployment. However, the Battalion Sergeant Major didn't approve of us at all and did what he could to shut us down. George was jumping through hoops to try and keep us going and even went as far as to get licensed as an official tattoo artist. The Battalion medics were coming in every week to inspect the room for cleanliness and to make sure that it was a sterile environment for health reasons. We were as legit as a real shop back in the States and we even had a chance to tattoo some of the Command guys from other units who couldn't believe we were about to be shut down. We officially got the word to close shop from our Battalion Sergeant Major and had to stop immediately. We were devastated but knew it was coming.

Rumors were beginning to go around that we were going to be extended from our current deployment time of one year to 15 months before we could go home and that we were going to be leaving Baghdad to another area of operations. We were furious that we were getting extended and I used this in my videos which pissed a lot of people off, but I didn't give a crap. I had a tool and decided to use it to blow off steam. I could feel the mentality changing in all the men in the Unit and especially myself. I was back to taking more pills to get to sleep and was beginning to get restless for action.

I was leaving my connex the other day and heard a loud explosion a few hundred meters away in our conned area and started to look for the nearest bunker, knowing that it was a mortar. I stood still listening for another round when I heard a hissing sound getting closer and closer and I froze in place. Time stopped and I started to think to myself that if I was going to get hit that there was nothing I could do about it and waited for the round to impact. The hissing stopped as a loud blast hit only a couple rows of rooms away from me. Dirt and decree fell all around me as I immediately ran for the area of the impact I didn't know what to expect but knew that someone could have been injured. I arrived near where the round landed and saw a lot of smoke filling the area and saw that it had landed right on someone's room. There were already soldiers surrounding the area and I ran up to offer my help.

Medics and other personnel were tearing through the completely destroyed room and I heard them yelling that there was no one in the room. I breathed with relief and started to look around for more damage. The mortar had destroyed everything inside including laptops, TVs, closets of uniforms and gear and all the equipment in the room. I learned that the two soldiers living there had just left to take their laundry to be cleaned. I didn't know it these guys were either very lucky or very unlucky because they had lost all their equipment and any letters and care packages they had gotten from the states.

There were shrapnel holes several convexes down from this one that only made it even more humbling to think that at any point we could be sleeping in our beds and one little piece of metal could come flying through the wall and take us out. Strangely though, this didn't bother me; what did I have to go home to? But even though it didn't really scare me I would still stop in place every time I heard a round coming in just to see where it would land or to see if this would be the one that found me. I wonder if anyone else did the same or if I was the only one.

12 December 2006, CPT Pike has moved on to bigger and better things and now we have CPT Torres. He came to us from Battalion with combat experience so we didn't have to worry about training up a new Commander, and he was eager to get in the fight. He was about my height; he too was of Hispanic decent so the ethnicity on our Stryker was pretty even. It was CPT Torres and Caz on the Hispanic side and myself and SSG Foster on the Caucasian sidewall I was actually on the Jew side, which many of my buddies had managed to crack a few jokes about. Every day we had managed to find at least one way to get a joke on each other and now had nicknames for each other. Foster, who we were calling Arthur by now, was the Bobble head, Reider was married to a Jew so he was Nate the Jew, Caz was still Caz, and I was Comanche Jew although Caz had unofficially made me an Honorary Mexican.

CPT Torres was too new to have a nick name and we really didn't think we would give him one. He liked to joke a lot pretending he was a Mexican Gangster and would cock his hat over and pretend to smoke a cigarette and speak using Mexican Slang and throw fake gang signs. He knew how to make us laugh but at the same time he was our new Company Commander so we had to keep it professional.

We never did play the song, Mad World after CPT Pike left. The song was number 22on my iPod so we started saying 220 to each other from them on. We welcomed CPT Torres to our small Stryker Family that we had made up of guys on our Stryker. We had become a pretty tight little group and often ran around the FOB together and even enjoyed a few barbeques on the FOB whenever we had the time. We would often hang out at the Tattoo Shop and move back and forth between our rooms to have hamburgers and Caz and his roommate, Sanchez, had gotten in good with the cooks at the chow hall and managed to get some steaks and fresh vegetables and we managed to have some pretty good cook outs.

The FOB life wasn't too bad although it was short lived. We got word that we were leaving our area and moving to New Baghdad south of Sadri City. The mission was to make Al Sadr think that we were planning an attack. We started to prep our gear and Strykers to move out and took the time to send emails and make phone calls because we were getting ready to live in our Strykers for a few days. All this was no shock but we had gotten comfortable in our area and I was pretty anxious to see some new territory. The days of patrolling to the RPG Alleys and the IP station were over.

My last memory of the IP station was sitting inside the compound walls at my gunner station when a small fire fight broke out with some insurgents on roof tops engaging the guard towers at the MP station. I remember looking straight up through my hatch watching tracers fly mere feet overhead. I was in awe of the site of red streams of light cracking above me, snapping as they passed by. It was like watching a science fiction movie and I could have almost climbed on top of my Stryker to lay down and watch it like a starry night. It reminded me of the Night Infiltration Course when I was in Basic Training when our whole Company of recruits were made to low crawl through mud and explosions to avoid getting hit by the rounds of tracers the Drill Sergeants were firing over us. It was a beautiful sight but it would be the last time in this area of operations when I would be in awe of such fire power.

CHAPTER 16
Fighting With Sticks and Stones

25 December 2006, Christmas a day of rejoice and getting to spend time with family and loved ones. The streets are filled with decorations and lights. In the snow covered streets back home a Christmas Day parade kicks off with the local high school marching bands, endless floats moving slowly along, and at the end a big float with Jolly Old St. Nick. For some it is a day to give and receive gifts and for many it is a day of celebrating the birth of Jesus Christ. Carolers move from house to house singing familiar Christmas tunes to all who would listen. Everyone back home is sending cards and care packages to us filled with gifts of beef jerky, wet wipes, gum, candy, chewing tobacco and cigarettes but we are not there to get them.

Today we have arrived in New Baghdad and we are to secure the area and support another Unit to the North. As we arrived we noticed several thousand people gathering in the city, screaming and waving red flags. We hadn't taken any contact yet so we figured it was just some unhappy demonstrators trying to scare us away. Our Stryker was moving behind an element from 3rd Platoon as we maneuvered through the tight alleys and streets and off to our left a group of about 100locals were gathered about 2meters from us when the unexpected happened. The 3rd Platoon Stryker in front of us had broken down in the middle of the fiasco. The Stryker had hit a large hole in the ground and snapped a drive shaft.

A couple squads dismounted to help hook the downed vehicle to the vehicle in front of them and another squad dismounted to keep the protestors from getting too close. I stood out of my hatch with CPT Torres with our rifles ready in case anyone got crazy. I watched a couple locals moving back and forth in front of the crowd with a large red flag and jumping at our soldiers on the ground trying to provoke us and the crowd at the same time. Sergeant Baker and Specialist Head, from 3rd Platoon were close to them and had to use non lethal rounds to deter the riled up ring leader but the crowd was getting louder and louder as the downed Stryker was finally hooked up. We started moving slowly back out of the alley towards the main route known as Predators. As we pulled out on to a larger road I heard a large roar of people right around the corner and it was confirmed when I finally made my way out on to the main street.

A crowd of thousands of people, adults and children alike, were marching towards our convoy chanting protests of anger towards the Americans being in their city. They were waving red flags and Iraqi flags and once they got within 5meters of us they began throwing rocks at our Strykers. This was only the beginning of what would be a very long standoff between us and the local people of New Baghdad and we hadn't seen the worst of it yet.

We finally made our way out to Route Predators and were directed to secure and block this route from any and all enemy activity as our brothers in the North hit their objective. My Stryker staged in the middle of the convoy facing south and I began to scan the surrounding crowds all around us. We had no reason to use any lethal force because they were mostly yelling and screaming with the occasional rock flying on to the top of my vehicle. I told Caz to keep an eye down the road but keep his hatch closed in case someone got close enough to throw a rock at him.

We watched as protestors started burning tires in the middle of the road and dragging large rocks out in the middle of it. I felt as if we had gone back in time to the days when men could only fight with sticks and rocks. The majority of the people in the city had gathered just North of our position near some wire that we had strong across the road to block them from coming to us. More rocks flew at me nearly hitting me in the head and now I was wishing I had a Sniper Netting like most of the other Strykers in our Company. The net was placed over the top of the Stryker so that no one could see us out of our hatches to keep from getting hit by sniper fire and now rocks. We hadn't gotten fitted with one before moving out to this city and the people were taking a lot of advantage of this.

We were still confident that nothing would get too serious because as loud and rough as this crowd could get we still have the bigger guns. We had smoke grenades, non-lethal ammunition, and if needed actual lethal rounds. We heard some commotion on the Battalion NET that a group of Humvees were moving through the crowds trying to get away from the people who were battering them with rocks. We didn't think it could be so bad but as the Humvees moved past us we could see all the thick glass on their trucks were nearly smashed and damaged. The situation was getting ugly and the Humvees were calling for assistance from us as they got closer to our wire obstacle.

CPT Torres had us turn our Stryker around so we could have eyes up the North to watch the Unit get through the crowd. I spotted two Humvees racing past the edge of the crowd and they had gotten caught up in the wire dragging it behind them when I spotted something tangled underneath the rear truck. It was a small boy who had got his leg wrapped in the wire and was being dragged down the asphalt road. The Humvees raced past my Stryker and I watched, in shock, as the small boy bounced underneath the chassis of the truck. Some dismounted soldiers spotted this and stopped the Humvees to try and untangle the boy. I could see them drag the kid out, his clothes were shredded and he was badly injured and bloody. He was unconscious as three local men ran to the boy. I assumed they were relatives and continued to watch as they picked the boy up and rushed him to a car. As the car sped off I dropped down into my Stryker and looked at CPT Torres, speechless. He could see the look of shock on my face and asked me what was wrong. Sir, I just watched to Humvees dragging a small boy down the road He knew it was going to get worse now that we had injured someone and ordered us to prepare for anything.

I jumped back out of my hatch with my rifle waiting for anything and the crowd was getting more agitated. The same little man that was exciting the smaller crowd in the alley was back and he had a look on his face that I knew would haunt me forever. It was as if he was strung out on some sort of drug or even demon possessed. It was like a scene from The Exorcist and I knew he was up to no good. He was at the lead of a crowd so large that it filled nearly every street around us. They were gathering rocks and anything they could pick up to use against us.

Behind the crowd we could see some M1 Tanks moving through them slowly so as to not run any one over and make the situation worse. We figured the tanks would scare the crowd away but the tanks weren't there to support us. They were running from the crowd who were pummeling them with large rocks. We got word on the NET to make a whole for them to pass through. They were running from the fight and this meant that the crowd was now our problem. As the tanks passed by we quickly closed up the gaps and began to block the roads but the crowd was beginning to surround our Strykers. We were ordered not to use lethal force and use non-lethal only but the crowd was so pumped up that non-lethal rounds weren't dispersing them. Then a breakthrough when we were given permission to use vehicle smoke grenades.

The Strykers in and around the crowd popped their

vehicle smoke into the crowd and almost immediately the streets were cleared. Once the crowd was split up we knew it was only a matter of time before the reconsolidated so we quickly spread out along the route and regained our sectors of fire, ready for anything. My Stryker was facing south again and for the next 1minutes we watched as the locals were slowly going away leaving a smaller group of people moving around the streets to the East and West. This could mean a lot of things; either they gave up and were trying to get back to their daily duties or they were trying to avoid the streets because there may be IEDs placed along the route and they don't want to be near them when they explode.

To my right I could see a tall building on the corner of the intersection with a man sitting outside a window just staring at our line of Strikers' decided to fix my RWS down that direction but he didn't move. I stood out of my hatch scanning the people and buildings looking for anything suspicious when I heard a loud bang and right in front of my face a bullet had impacted on the armor of my Stryker. I quickly dropped in my hatch and stared at the screen of my FCU hoping to spot a Sniper and my heart began racing very quickly and once again CPT Torres asked me what was wrong. Sir, a freaking sniper damn near took my freaking head off! I wanted to start firing my .5cal on the whole crowd but he quickly told me to hold fire. I went back to the window where I had spotted a man before but he was gone. I thought that maybe he had been sitting there waiting for me to drop my guard to take a shot by the Iraqi interpreter riding on my Stryker quickly told me to scan my RWS on to a car that was racing away. There goes your Sniper, shoot him! I didn't have a positive ID and I knew that if I tried to shoot I would end up wiping out a large number of locals and CPT Torres had already ordered me to hold fire. There were a lot of women and children moving around as if nothing had happened even though I knew they heard the shot.

Earlier today when we had first moved on to Route Predators different elements from the Company were taking Sniper fire from a house and I had even gone as far as to put my helmet on a stick and lift it up out of the hatch to try and draw fire so we could spot where it was coming from. I wasn't the only one that tried this, 3rd Platoons Platoon Leader had tried the same thing as the Sniper continued to take shots at a large number of us and the closest he had got was to one of our Tanker guys.

We were now waiting for anything, as we all scanned our sectors along the route. We suspected that we were about to start hearing IED explosions so we had a group of Engineer Humvees move along the route to clear it of IEDs. One Humvee was hit on their way south and a piece of metal had hit the young soldier fatally wounding him and after that they had not spotted any more bombs.

It was getting later in the afternoon and we were already sick of sitting on this route waiting to be attacked at any time. It was Christmas and our moral was already nonexistent when we got more bad news. Brigade wanted us to sit on this route and keep it secure for the remainder of the night. I was already pretty jumpy after a Sniper had damn near got me and I could feel my heart start to beat faster with anger. Why us? I asked, Why do we always get stuck with these bullcrap missions?! CPT Torres looked at me and reassured me that everything would be o.k. looked to the left of my FCU at the tiny fake Christmas tree my mom had sent me in the mail that I had fastened with some zip ties and the only words I could think to say were, screw Christmas!

As the sun began to go down below the horizon we decided to push the Snipers and other dismounts out to some surrounding roof tops as the vehicles restaged along the route. My Stryker pushed north towards the end of our line and a few other Strykers were told to drive up and down the route to try and keep anyone from placing IEDs under the cover of night. We didn't think it was a possibility because we had thermal sites and could clearly see everything that was going on around us.

We sat in our position and scanned almost as soon as it got completely dark our patrolling vehicles from 1st Platoon began getting hit by small IEDs. No one had been injured but a couple Strykers were temporarily disabled in the blast. They assessed the damage and continued moving. Not too long after they started moving again they were attacked by another IED. We quickly realized that even though we had the road completely covered and were patrolling, one or more insurgents were moving behind the Strykers and emplacing small IEDs and moving away before they were spotted. We had to change our game plan and started scanning more than patrolling.

One of our Stryker Vehicle Commanders spotted a hot spot near a traffic circle along the route and we set up a small security element on the area and called EOD to investigate. For the next hour or so we watched as the EOD robot moved on to the hot spot and confirmed it to be a small Edythe robot sat a small brick of C4 explosives on the spot and dragged a line of detonator chord back to where the EOD vehicle was staged. The call came over the net to ensure all personnel were clear of the area and that our hatches were all buttoned up. BOOM A small shock wave came across the streets waking up some men that were sleeping on the sidewalk near the blast. The sight of the blast in our thermal cameras was awe inspiring and I managed to get some video footage of the blast to save for later.

I don't know if we had scared the personnel emplacing the IEDs or if they realized that we had caught on to their plan but for the rest of the night we saw little movement of any kind and went back to scanning the area. This was our Christmas and all I could think about for the rest of the night as I scanned was how nice it would be to be back in the States eating a nice fattening home cooked meal. How nice it must have been for everyone back home to be exchanging gifts and watching Christmas movies on TV.I ripped my tiny Christmas tree from the zip ties that held it in place and through it out of my hatch on to the street outside screaming to everyone that lived in New Baghdad, Merry Christmas you idiots! I am not sure if anyone heard me and I hoped that I had woke someone up and I looked at CPT Torres staring at me and we both started laughing at my silly display of frustration. This was our Christmas Vacation our holiday with the family.

On this dark city street in the middle of New Baghdad, we were having our Christmas Dinners. We opened our MREs and said a Merry Christmas to each other as we ate and pulled security. I had a moment of complete peace and for that moment I was thankful to be with such awesome brothers for this holiday. This was my home and I was with my family and I knew that if I ever made it out of this crap hole alive I would never forget this night.

26 December 2006, we finally got to move off of Route Predators to a place known as The Cigarette Factory. It was a large area of giant spools of material spread out across a walled in field. There were larger buildings that the dismounts were clearing as the Strykers pulled security around the perimeter. Along one side 1st Platoon started taking small arms fire and insurgents were tossing grenades over the wall trying to hit them

but was unsuccessful.CPT Torres had us pull the Stryker to the area where 1st Platoon was but as soon as we got there the firing ended.

Hours later the buildings were finally cleared and we began staging to move out. We were all in line and I had Caz pull our Stryker in behind a 1st Platoon Stryker and the entire Company began moving out. The route was littered with garbage and piles of junk so we had to move slow and keep our eyes open for IEDs. We were moving past some damaged houses on our right and it got very quiet all of the sudden. Then, I heard a blast and saw smoke in between our Stryker and the Stryker in front of us. A small IED had hit and I immediately scanned to the right and there standing about 25 meters from my Stryker was an adult male holding a detonator connected to wire that ran right to our position Sir, he has got a freaking detonator in his hand! I yelled to CPT Torres and he replied, Well freaking shoot him! I quickly armed my .5cal and squeezed the trigger and within seconds I had nearly cut the man in half before he had a chance to run

I couldn't stop firing I just watched round after round strike his body and everything around him Nearly every other Stryker behind us with a .5cal decided to add some suppression to the area The entire action lasted about 1seconds but it seemed like several minutes we couldn't believe that I scanned right on to the guy and cut him down before he had a chance to run. It was crazy that the guy was standing right in the open holding the detonator but I didn't give a crap, he might have had a second detonator ready to set off another IED.I got some congratulations from the guys in the Stryker and we continued moving.

We left New Baghdad feeling a little stronger and still in a state of shock at what we had been through these last couple days. Over the course of these couple days we had watched crowds of people chasing Humvees and Tanks away with rocks, I saw a small boy dragged through the streets like a rag doll. We experienced multiple IEDs and EFPs that were being emplaced right under our noses. We watched a bold man standing only 25 meters away from us try to blow us up with a small IED and I watched that same man get cut in half by my own machine gun firewall in all we headed back to FOB Liberty with a little more experience and we were very anxious to get back in to familiar territory. Was this the worst thing we would experience here? Is it possible that maybe next time we would be the ones running from crowds with rocks? Never We were Comanche Company and nobody could ever make us run.

CHAPTER 17
A New Year

1 January 2007, another year has passed by us. Comanche Company 1/23 Infantry has seen and done more than anyone could ever imagine. We have made friends and we have lost friends. We have shared experiences that will live with us for the rest of our lives, some good and some bad. We have traveled from the other side of the world to this place that some of us now call home. Nothing can erase our experiences and the images of these times will forever be embedded in our minds like a bad horror movie.

Thousands of miles away our friends and families are living their lives, working their jobs, paying their bills, going to dinners, parties and celebrating the New Year and in their busy lives they manage to take time to put together letters and care packages to send to us. We have had a few days to spend back on the FOB trying to relax as much as possible. We have started to do more patrolling in our old area of operations and in our down time we have gotten a chance to write letters and emails to home.

The Battalion Commander has decided to allow us to start the tattoo shop back up but the funds that we make are to be used for a party when we get home. We are also supposed to continue getting weekly inspections from the medics for cleanliness and we are only allowed to give tattoos to members of our Battalion. Baghdad Ink is officially open for business and we are all pretty excited about it.

For us this New Year is just another day when we get a chance to eat some special food that the cooks have prepared in the chow hall and although we don't get to drink alcohol we did manage to take a bunch of bottles of grape juice and cider back to our rooms. Everyone at home is watching the ball drop in Times Square as we listen to explosions outside the FOB and even a few mortars that have managed to land inside the FOB.

I got a chance to make my way around our Company area and take some pictures of the guys from our unit doing the usual crazy jokes on each other like staging fake ambushes on their squad leaders kidnapping them and holding them hostage inside their rooms to see if other squad members would try and rescue them.3rd Platoon is notorious for this; they have a few guys that dress up like terrorists and hide underneath their metal rooms waiting for unsuspecting leaders to be nabbed.

We also had a chance to do some much needed maintenance on our Strykers and me and Caz have spent a lot of time with the mechanics in the motor pool trying to get our Stryker running like new although we still haven't gotten the armor replaced from when our vehicle was hit by an IED months ago. The mechanics are pretty good about hooking us up and they made us a cage to mount on top of our Stryker for our Sniper Netting which I have grown quite fond of since it not only keeps us a little safer from enemy fire but it also provides us with a decent amount of shade.

I am not sure what this next year will bring us but we already pretty much know that the rumors of our extension are true. Instead of being here for only 12 months we will be here for a total of 15 months. We were mad about it for a while but don't really have a choice but to drive on and continue mission as usual. hats the great thing about our job is that we are trained to be flexible. Although we bitch and complain we know we can't change it so we might as well go along with it.

24 January 2007, We moved towards a small urban area with a main street running through it known as Haifa Street. We had gotten word that locals there were being run out of their homes and we were to move in to try and help regain the area that has already been a known hot spot for Anti Iraqi activity. Almost instantly, as we moved on to the street, insurgents started throwing grenades from the rooftops on either side of the tiny alley we were in. Because it was such a tight area we couldn't move left or right to stay away from the grenades we had to close our hatches and let the Stryker armor take the blows.

At the end of the street there were several high rise buildings that were perfect for enemy Snipers to take shots at us and along with help from Bravo Company our guys had to clear the entire buildings to gain a foot hold on the enemy. On the opposite end of the street where we were entering was a large traffic circle in front of a large gate into a cemetery.CPT Torres had us stage our Stryker at the base of the traffic circle facing the high rise buildings to cover our dismounts as they entered the tall buildings.

Up the street from us a few other Strykers staged with groups of Iraqi Army Soldiers in front of a small mosque that we suspected the enemy was hiding in. Off to my right was a set of two story buildings that I decided to use as my sector of fire and almost as soon as we sat in we started taking RPG fire from nearby alleys and Caz spotted muzzle flash from a window near where I was scanning. I quickly scanned to the window and spotted the flash and I started hearing the pinging sounds of enemy rounds hitting the front of our Stryker so I opened fire. As soon as I did a group of Strykers off to my left opened up on the buildings next to the one I was firing on and started reporting enemy fire from further down the street.

I looked at what they were talking about and could see the entrance to an alley that had been built up by sand bags almost like a make shift bunker that Hajj was using for cover. I quickly began suppressing that area at the same time I would move my weapon back on to the window. I started spotting more than just muzzle flash and could see the guy that was shooting at us and I reengaged the window immediately taking the guy out. As soon as that guy went down another took his place These suckers have balls, sir When one gets messed up another takes his place! I yelled to CPT Torres and he said to keep firing This went on for nearly an hour and we were taking a lot of fire from these two positions. Finally we got a request from the Tanker section to pull up and engage the building with a TOW missile. After a few minutes of trying to get permission from Battalion we finally got the green light and an ATGM pulled forward. We slowed our rates of fire down to a minimum while the ATGM got his sites on the building. I heard a pop and a loud hissing sound and I saw the missile fly across the street hitting the building on the side leveling much of the wall

We waited as the smoke cleared and the enemy firing had stopped. Either the missile had killed everyone inside the building or scared the crap out of them because we didn't hear a single round come from that building. The Iraqi Army Soldiers up the street then started taking fire from around the mosque and immediately started firing with their AK-47s and RPGs Almost immediately the Stryker near them started getting hit with small arms from the opposite side of the street that the IA was shooting at. I watched as the Stryker was shooting over the heads of the IA and the IA was shooting over the top of the Stryker at the mosque It was an awesome site to watch them trust each other enough to stay where they were and suppress their targets.

The Stryker stopped firing and reported that they had destroyed the enemy targets but the IA was still taking fire from the mosque. We knew we had to get in that mosque and take those losers out There was no real way to get into the mosque because the thick metal doors were tightly locked so the IA decided they would try to breach the walls with an RPG. The firing finally stopped giving one of them a chance to step to a safe distance and fired an RPG at the side of the wall. As the dust settled we could see that it had no affect on the wall only leaving a small spot of black on it. The same soldier stepped back out to try again but once again it had no effect.

We pulled one of our ATGMs up to try and make a whole with a missile and after reporting that they were going to fire we watched the round fly from the top of the Stryker to the wall and we heard the loud boom and a large ball of smoke and fire shot out from the impact. Nothing. The ATGM failed to get within arming distance and was too close for the missile to have any affect. So they backed the ATGM as far as they could up to the edge of a sidewalk and fired again this time the rocket had distance enough to arm and we saw a much larger ball of fire this time but once again, nothing. The walls of the building were so thick that even our missiles couldn't penetrate so the ATGM Commander decided to try and find another spot to breach.

Around the corner was a large steal door leading in to the mosque and they decided that this would be their best chance at getting in to the mosque. The ATGM quickly repositioned and fired one more round with success this time. A large shockwave moved across the street and we saw a large piece of steel door fly high up into the air and come crashing down below. Now was our chance to send some guys into the mosque but not until the Iraqi Army moved in first.

Far at the end of the street in the high rise buildings a platoon from Bravo Company was clearing with a news team following and interviewing soldiers along the way. A squad from their company was clearing a room when suddenly a cry for help came from one of the rooms. The news team filmed the entire time as a soldier cried from in the room that one of their squad members had been hit by a sniper round. They quickly moved into action and had to evacuate the wounded soldier from the scene as the film crew caught everything on tape. A stream of the man's blood streaked across the room as the rest of the team tried to secure his weapon and gear.
SSG Hector Leiha had been fatally wounded that day and the fire fight continued for 15 hours as machine guns, air support

and mortar rounds destroyed several enemy positions around the city. By the end of the mission the entire city became a ghost town. If there were any enemy forces still alive they were long gone and the city was declared safe again.

We moved back to the FOB quickly and quietly and as leaders gathered together they began laying out the story board and discussing all that had happened in complete detail. One of the guys in the CP began scanning the internet to see if anything had been said about the mission in the news. Not even a few hours after we were back there were special reports and news broadcasts showing video of the whole thing on nearly every major news channel. All the fighting, explosions and even footage of the Bravo Company squad that lost one of their own was all over the internet. We watched in shock at what was being showed to the world back home. I remember thinking that I hoped no one I cared about was watching and because of the loss our Battalion took we weren't allowed to use our phones or internet so as to not leak any information, but we didn't have to. The whole thing was there for the world to see and I could hardly believe I was part of it.

28 January 2007, Over the course of the last few weeks we have had some down time but have spent most of our time outside the wire chasing ghosts. We get several tips coming in from local Iraqi citizens with information leading us to suspected terrorists and activities. When they call in tips that lead us to something they usually get a reward for their information, which leads to a lot of running around from house to house looking for people who usually aren't there.

One day we were out running through alley after alley chasing a tip that we had gotten which finally led us to one single house. As dismounts entered the house they found it completely empty except that it had been rigged with explosives. We had been led into a trap but luckily we got out before it exploded and we left it for DOD to handle. Hajj was starting to use the tips as bate to bring us into a whole new trap which is now known as a HBIED (House Born IED).

On our way back one of our Strykers was hit by an EFP. Luckily no one was hurt but it left a hole in the side of the Stryker that went all the way through the engine compartment and out the other side.SSG Sager was in command of the vehicle and he took some shrapnel in his arm but was fine other than that. Once again we were shown how much we were not in control of anything we were trying to accomplish. I am thankful that no one was seriously hurt but when is it going to be enough? Will the next man be so lucky? Several years after Saddams capture and now he is dead but we are still here.

I am going on leave soon but will I make it that longhand even if I do make it to that day will I want to go? So many questions running through my mind through all our minds. This is going to be a long war.

CHAPTER 18
Back From Leave

15 March 2007, I am back from leave and I have never really felt so out of place in my life. My friend Wes picked me up and we spent some time together in Missouri and even took a trip to Kansas to see a famous car from one of our favorite movies. I also got to see my sister, Sara, who I haven't seen in a very long time.

It's odd that my sister and I grew up and were always very close. We always looked out for each other and being only three years apart we were usually in the same school so we had plenty of time together. But when I saw her I didn't know how to act around her or anyone else for that matter. I was back in the United States but I felt far away from home. I was in a strange world where not everyone hated me or wanted to kill me and it was quite uncomfortable.

Over the period of the couple weeks that I was there I got to visit a few people but for the most part I stayed at my mother's house and did my best to keep an eye on the news or the internet in case anything happened to my friends who were still fighting. I would never forgive myself if anything happened to them. I stayed up late hoping to catch one of them online just to get updates and they were fine for the most part.

I spent a lot of time with Wes and his wife but I was burning up inside just waiting to get back on the plane to my brothers. I stayed drunk for damn near the entire time I was there just to keep my anger and pain as numb as possible but it wasn't working. Wes had to pull me out of the house one night because I started burning my arm with a cigarette leaving seven burn spots one for each kill. Everyone there was very scared that night, including my sister and by the time I realized what I was doing I quickly put out the cigarette and began to confess to my friend that I was scared to be there. I didn't know how to act and when he finally brought me back to the house I did my best to reassure my sister that I would be ok and we all finally went to bed.

I was so messed up while I was there that I couldn't even face my father and brother. I had a younger brother that was born just before I joined the Army that I have never even met and I should them up because I was scared to leave the house. I was safe there with no civilians or crowds and even though I knew nothing would happen I didn't want to risk it. The time that I actually did get out of the house I was so busy scanning windows and rooftops for enemy that I didn't get a chance to see the sights of the town I grew up in.

The day finally came for me to leave and I remember slowly climbing on to a shuttle van to go back to the airport. Some of my friends were there to say good bye and I looked back at them one last time and put up a peace sign with my hand as the door closed. Was this the last time I would see them? Did I waste my entire leave drinking and worrying about my friends on the other side of the world? But more importantly, would I ever see my friends in Missouri again? They were all so kind and patient with me and I hoped that I didn't hurt anyone because of my own issues. But it was too late and as the van pulled away for the airport I put on my headphones and spent the trip with my eyes closed trying to hide any emotions or from the other people traveling with me. I was going back to my boys, my home.

27 March 2007, I am long since back from leave and Missouri is a distant memory now. A lot has happened and more has changed. We really haven't made any progress except we are starting to see learn how things really are behind the curtains.

The Shiia Iraqi Army Forces are forming rogue groups and wait for us to do any neighborhood clearing and come into our battle space with false blacklists of random Sunni men. Then without us being able to interdict they take these men into custody and they are never heard from again. We predict they are forming these groups as part of their ethnic cleansing. The Shiia and Sunni have been fighting for many years and now the neighborhoods are torn by religious indifference. The crappy thing about it is that we can't do anything about it. We can't pick sides with the Shiia or the Sunni and if we work with any of them then we are aiding the enemy of the other side. These rogue groups have also been known to set IEDs against coalition forces.

One rogue group is led by and Iraqi Lieutenant Colonel and we have had problems with him before. Only a couple days ago we had a run-in with his group when they came looking for a young man who was supposedly on their blacklist and as they detained him we tried to take photographs and gather information on the man to check our own sources and they wouldn't let us. My Stryker was stopped in an intersection when this was going down and the Iraqi Lieutenant Colonel and his men were stopped in an Iraqi Humvee with a machine gun mounted on top.

There were dismounts from another one of our Companies and CPT Torres was dismounted to aid in trying to gather information from the LTC. I remember watching the LTCs men watching us like they wanted to fight and the LTC was being very shady. He refused to give up any information and started to yell at us and next thing we know everyone had a weapon drawn on one another. The men in the Iraqi Humvee turned their weapons on us and the large machine gun on top was pointed right into the middle of where our dismounts were standing CPT Torres and the men on the ground finally got everyone calmed down and we began to clear the area letting the Iraqi LTC get away with the man they detained knowing full-well that he was about to be executed for his religious beliefs.

A small group from our section decided that we wouldn't let this happen anymore and we set up a secret point in our perimeter to let the Sunni families exit out of the city before they were captured by the Rogue Shiia. We weren't taking sides but we weren't about to watch families torn apart and executed without mercy or the chance to defend themselves. We were trying to give them democracy and in the hard heads of the Iraqi people they would rather live in tyranny and murder. I really don't see them changing at allot for us.

I don't know what good we can possibly do for these people when they would rather live this way. It's been like this for too long and I really believe, as sad as it is to admit, that the murdering will continue on both sides of the fence here. Once again we have to choose mission over morals so we fight on and we just keep on fighting each other. I think I am going to put down the journal for a while. I really don't feel much like remember too much more of this although I don't know how much it will help. I don't have to write anything down here for it to burn into my brain.

2April 2007, I am leaving the unit. Not by choice, I would never leave my brothers alone on purpose, but when I reenlisted in Kuwait I wanted to be stabilized which means I would get to stay with 1/23 Infantry no matter how many more times they deploy, but when I signed the contract I didn't know that it said, needs of the Army meaning I don't have a choice in what I do. I have to report to Fort Benning, GA almost as soon as we get back from the deployment and since we got extended that means more time with my brothers. I don't know how I will handle it, my First Sergeant says it's a good thing for me to go because it will give me a break from being a grunt and give me time to heal from my wounds.

I really don't feel that I need a break and would rather just go back with my boys and keep training for the next tour. But as crappy as I feel this is I will make the most of it and do my best no matter what it is I will be doing. Most likely, since I have the experience, I will be a Stryker Instructor and train other soldiers to do what I do as a Stryker Vehicle Commander. I don't know the full details but I will do my best because orders are orders.

CHAPTER 19
Missing In Action

14 May 2007, A couple of nights ago 2 Humvees from another unit decided to head out and was ambushed. A nearby unit heard explosions and tried to raise them on the NET with no response and called QRF. Once they arrived they found two burning Humvees and three or four bodies leaving three MIA (Missing in Action).Our Company along with Bravo Company were called to assist in the search in the remote city and the surrounding area.

The city and surrounding villages are mostly farm land and large open fields cut off by a large creek making the search quite difficult because if they were captured they could be in any house, left in the creek or even buried somewhere.

We stayed inside one of the little COPs (Combat Outposts) to use as a Command Post and the searches would continue from there. Our Company broke into different sections with dismounts going out every few hours in Blackhawks Helicopters to get into the areas that our Strykers couldn't get to. For the rest of us we would travel down remote roads and do our search that way.

We have been searching now for two days and yesterday, Mothers Day, we were searching some houses and traveling down a road paralleling the large creek exposing us to a lot of wood lines that could be used as avenues of approach. Dismounts walked along with the Strykers as they traveled and with CPT Torres on the ground it left Caz, myself and Arthur in the rear air guard hatch scanning the wooded areas.

We stopped momentarily to check a couple houses on our left and to our right was a large amount of woods and thick brush and I heard a loud metal on metal bang on the right side of my Stryker Instantly Arthur began to yell out that we were getting shot at and a couple of rounds had already flown near his head Check the wood line to our right! Arthur yelled as he returned fire with his M4 Carbine. I quickly scanned to the right and immediately spotted the heat signature of a single man with an AK-47.He was approximately 10meters away and I began firing into the wood line at his position!

I called up the contact to CPT Torres and I had Caz pull the nose of the Stryker to point at the man so we weren't exposed to any more flank shots in case he had an RPG.As soon as we did I started firing again and the shooting stopped. I scanned to where the man was and saw the heat from his body lying in the brush. I am not sure if Arthur got him or I did but we chalked it up as a successful kill for the both of us and I continued to scan the area for any follow-on attacks.

Arthur was pretty excited about it and a little shook up because he could have been shot in the head had the man been a little more accurate with his shots. The Sniper netting we had put up covered a lot of the area around the air guard hatches but we had cut out a small window to make room for our rifle of an M24machine gun and we suspect the man spotted Arthur through that window. That time Arthur and I became a little better friends and I knew if we got out of this alive we would be drinking beers together for life.

We took a lot more contact that day from enemy moving around the wooded areas and firing at the dismounts from 1st Platoon. My best friend, Cody, was on the ground that day and I had to pull a lot of support for them while they were dismounted but the enemy knew that area a lot better than we did so they knew exactly where to hide.

We spotted a couple IEDs on the road but since we were pinned between the creek and a high bank on our left we couldn't go around them so we called EOD up with their trucks to disarm the bombs and one of them was even hit damaging the steering wheels. We stayed on that road for hours trying to get the damaged vehicles recovered and back for repairs. I could only pray that these men were found soon because we were up against local enemy and we knew they had the advantage against us in these remote areas.

Arthur and I bragged about it back at the COP and Reider was even excited because he got to fire his weapon. Despite the fact that Reider was always out with us this was his first time getting some real action. We all had our moments of celebration because none of our guys was actually hurt but we knew what we were there for. There were American soldiers lost out there and we had to find them. It was like finding a needle in a haystack but we knew we had to do our best no matter what.

Back at the COP I built a makeshift living area out of a couple ponchos and chord to give us shade and we nicknamed it The Swamp after a popular old war show called M.A.S.H.CPT Torres loved it and we spent most of our down time in The Swamp drinking more energy drinks and talking about home. No matter where we were, we always managed to find a way to make it feel like home or at least a little more comfortable.

After several days of searches we found several clues leading us closer to finding the missing Soldiers including tips from locals and the ID card of one of them far away in another city. A lot of questions were being raised as to what happened the night they were ambushed and Blackhawks were dropping flyers around the area to offer rewards to anyone with information.

Money drives a lot of the people in Iraq because of the poverty. A lot of the IEDs and attacks on us were coming from people with poor families who were hired by the enemy for a couple hundred dollars to emplace and set off IEDs and take shots at us with rifles and RPGs. We knew we could use this to our advantage and a large cash reward would be given to anyone with information leading us to the missing soldiers. These were desperate times for us and we were trying everything we could to find them.

25 May 2007, Today was our last day of searching. We found one body several kilometers south from where we were looking. I feel for the families of these men as the search will continue without us. So many days of searching without out much luck at all, I can't imagine what this unit is feeling knowing that they have brothers out there somewhere. I hope and pray that they will be found and for the family and loved ones of the soldier that was found I hope that they realize that their soldier died a hero.

As for us, we have gotten word that we are heading back to prepare for our final mission in Iraq; we are going to Baqubah. I don't know much about it except it's pretty rough territory and full of Deep Buried IEDs. The end is so near and yet so far out of reach and I hope that we all make it through it alive.

CHAPTER 20
Getting Ready For Baqubah

1 June 2007, we are getting some down time again back on FOB Liberty and Caz and I are taking the time to prepare the Stryker for our last big mission. We are going to Baqubah and so far all we know is that it's going to be a long trip away from the FOB. We don't know about the living conditions or how the people will welcome us, we just know that the units there have been having a lot of trouble securing their area. I don't like to talk crap about other units, but it seems like we get called up to do a lot of clean-up for other units. I was talking to my buddy the other day and his company is making T-shirts that say, We came here to do our job and ended up doing yours On the back it has all the patches of the units that we have gone to help. We laughed about it and I am sure it will cause a lot of stink with other units, but we really don't give a crap.

Baghdad Ink is back in action; George, Mikey and I are still giving and getting a lot of tattoos but packing up some of the equipment to send back. We are planning a Closing Party with all the guys that hang out at the shop as kind of a goodbye to the good times we had in the shop. We have some civilian buddies there on the FOB that have the hook-up for some booze so we hope it will be a memorable party. We have to be very careful because the Battalion Commander and Command Sergeant Major has had his eye on a lot of us for finding and consuming alcohol so it will be a hush-hush get together.

I have been spending more time hanging out with Arthur and he has introduced me to a friend of his wife's back home. I have been chatting online with Arthurs friend, Mindy, and seems we have hit it off pretty quickly. We have a lot in common but I think she is standing off a little bit because of what I do for a living.

I find myself staying up until 3 or 4 in the morning just talking to her about anything and everything. I don't have the guts to call her yet, but I am sure I will. Arthur keeps bugging me to call her but I am a bit shy and since my last relationship ended so badly I have my own walls up. But Mindy seems to be able to find a lot of ways to get me to open up.

I met her friend, Tay, online the other night and it didn't take me long to get in good with her. Tay is a little vulgar...ok she is a lot vulgar, and by the end of the conversation we were calling each other fart knocker and threatening to fart on each other the first time we meet. Tay is her roommate and I am sure that if I and Mindy decide to hang out I will meet her. There is just something about this girl that I can't get enough of and even though we have a big mission to get through we are already making plans to get together.

My buddy, Ian, is helping me buy a car and the only way to do it is if I transfer $7000 into Mindy's account and have her pick it up for me. She said she would do it and for me to trust her with this money is pretty scary. Arthur said she is a good girl and I have nothing to worry about.

I am planning on putting the journal down for a while since nothing really ever happens on the FOB while we are prepping for a mission. I will start putting more entries in when we are in Baqubah.

CHAPTER 21
Baqubah

1June 2007, we rolled in to Baqubah on a main road and instead of stopping to set up our living quarters we decided to roll straight into the surge. Our Company moved in the Strykers down a main route to one side of the city and stopped on line. Caz pulled the front of the Stryker to the right and we started scanning. Not a soul in sight and we could already see the damage in the city caused by previous units obviously getting into some pretty heavy fighting. There were holes in almost every building and every wall. Some of the buildings had entire walls missing from mortar rounds and air support.

Instead of risking an ambush we started to pop vehicle smoke into the grassy area in front of us that separated us from the houses. There really wasn't much cover so we had to try and conceal the movement of our dismounts as best as we could. I armed and fired my smoke and I watched the canister fly up into the air exploding in a bright flash and then a smoky haze began to settle. Hot bits of White Phosphorus dropped to the grass immediately lighting small fires in the dry grass.

It was just getting light out in the early morning when we arrived so the fires were brighter and a small nearby tree began to catch fire. The dismounts began to jump out of the back of the Strykers and they also through smoke to help conceal their movement. We don't know enough about this place to risk getting an attack from the buildings and we knew we would be here for a while so the extra smoke was a help.

I looked out of my hatch to take a couple pictures and what I saw made my eyes widen. Large fires were beginning to spread and there were several different colors of smoke spreading across the streets around our vehicles. This is how we started our last mission. We wanted to make in immediate impression on the people here with a show of force so every Stryker and every soldier was on the ground. An entire Battalion of Tomahawks were here in force and we were going to take care of this place as quickly as possible.

2June 2007, We finally stopped the first wave of assault and we started a rotation of Platoons who would stay out and clear and the rest would go back to FOB Warhorse for chow and rest. Since we were with the Commanders Stryker we knew that nearly every time a Platoon was out we would be with them, but managed to get some time back in the rear to get some air conditioner.

We were put up in 3 large tents near the chow hall. We didn't need much but we were lucky to have electricity and a phone to call home when we had a break. Some of the Battalion guys were in the same tent as us and they had a TV with a Play station set up for entertainment. Every time we came back to rest we had to put up with the loud TV and they were always yelling but all I had to do was put on my headphones and relax.

My iPod had the ability to keep pictures on it so I would flip through them as I listened to music. I had some pictures that Mindy had sent to me of her back home with her friends and it was nice to see a pretty face. She has really got me thinking but I am still a little nervous to call. Arthur continues to bug me about it and I think it's about time to call. I don't know why I am so nervous we have already talked so much on the internet that I feel like I know her. I have already called a couple times but the conversations never really lasted because I had a prepaid cell phone and it was costly but the phone in the tent was free.

Mindy is not like any girl I have ever dated. The first thing I noticed about her was her red hair. I have always had a thing for red heads plus she is a shorter girl and I like short girls too. She is a very open and charismatic person and I have always enjoyed coming back from a mission and seeing a new email from her. She would often email me from her work and I remember she said that she would sometimes catch hell from her boss for it. I always liked staying up late and talking to her. So why should I say no to calling her when I know I want to talk to her. Screw it I will call her while I am here, God knows when I will get another chance since we are running long hours outside the FOB.

21 June 2007, the surge continued today and we moved further into the city but we had to stop at an intersection because the road we needed to go down was rumored to have Deep Buried IEDs. The Engineers have something called a MICLIC. It is loaded on a trailer that's pulled behind their vehicles and, when used properly, fires from the back and shoots across a mine field or road and has several charges on it. When it is spread out across an area the entire thing detonates and sets off any mines or Deep Buried IEDs in its path clearing it for us to move through the danger zone.

Our vehicle staged out of the way but in a good position to use security and waited for the engineers to fire the MICLIC on to the road. Normal procedure is for them to set the charges and then call us up with enough warning for us to button up inside the Stryker, however we didn't get a warning and CPT Torres, myself and Arthur were outside of the hatches when it detonated about 5meters from us The Stryker shook as a large ball of smoke and debris surrounded us knocking us down into the hatches My heart began racing thinking that we had been hit by an RPG or someone was hit by an IED close by.

Immediately, the Engineers called up that they had set of the MICLIC and they were going to clear the road of any other IEDs. We all looked at each other and started laughing when we realized what had happened. It was louder than when I was hit by the IED and the power of the MICLIC was unlike anything I had been close to. It was exciting but we were pissed that we didn't get the warning but luckily no one was hurt.

We repositioned back in to the intersection and a couple other Strykers were on either side of us. To our 1 o'clock was what seemed to be an abandoned building on the corner and behind it was a housing area much like housing areas back in the States. Inside it was a road through the middle and a cul-de-sac and the area would be a great place to set in an OP (Observation Post) but the area had to be cleared first. CPT Torres called in all the PLs (Platoon Leaders) to our Stryker to come up with a plan on how to clear the area which was almost directly in the center of the area we were clearing.

The plan was set and before we could start clearing we started taking pot shots from a window of the building on the corner. We returned fire but no one could get a good angle on the building so we called up air support to hit it. Quickly an Apache Attack Helicopter responded with a quick blast from its guns and a Hellfire missile. I got some good video of the whole thing through my RWS camera and the firing from the building stopped. We were set to move in to the housing area and it soon became our new little home away from home during our long hours from the FOB.

We settled our Stryker along with another Platoon inside and began a quick clearing of all the houses and found them abandoned. Whoever lived here before us was either scared away from all the fighting or was forced out of their homes by Anti-Iraqi Forces. We decided to chill there for a bit and another Platoon had gone back to the FOB to grab a bunch of boxed hot meals for us to eat while we rested. It was a simple plan for us;

some of the other platoons would clear and hold an area while the rest of us relaxed inside the OP. This made it easier for us since our Battalion Command wanted constant presence in the city to make it less likely for enemy to sneak in to the area.

We got some rest and moved back out to the intersection to pull security down the long road until the area we were assigned was cleared. About 150meters down the long road was another intersection that was close to a section from our 2nd Platoon but I began so see something moving. I zoomed in with my thermal camera as far as I could and saw 3 personnel moving around corners of buildings and bushes toward our position. I reported it to the 2nd Platoon element that had holed up in a house to observe but they couldn't get eyes on what I was seeing. CPT Torres said to fire some warning shots down the road so I checked to make sure there weren't any friendly forces in the area and opened up with a small burst of my .50cal.

The personnel immediately ducked for cover and a few moments later began moving towards us again. The closer they got the more I could see they were carrying something in their hands. I couldn't be sure what it was but if it was friendly they would know better than to keep moving. It's not unusual to see women and children walking around because they are so used to American forces and they weren't scared until firing started. I continued to observe and report until finally I could tell that they were carrying weapons and got the clearance to fire.

I put my reticule center mass of the personnel and pulled the trigger Several loud thumps came from my .5cal and hot brass fell down into my hatch on top of my head I watched the rounds impact all around them and a large ball of dust consumed them as I let off about 15 rounds. I let off the trigger and observed the area as the dust settled and could see bits of hot spots all around where they were.2nd Platoon adjusted their position to observe where I was firing and saw no more movement. Got three more Caz! I announced to my driver through the head seethe good job man! he responded. And as soon as he said that I shoved it in the back of my mind to think about later when I had the time. I never really stop to think after I engage an enemy, I don't want to think about them being human and having family. It's that kind of crap that gets you killed here or worse; getting one of your buddies killed. I am sure if I make it out of here alive I will have to deal with it but for now I will get back to the mission as usual. I assume that this is what most of our guys do in this situation.

22 June 2007,I left Caz on the FOB last night for this long stretch of missions. He never complains but I know he is tired and the heat here is unbearable at times. Inside the drivers hatch of a Stryker can reach temperatures over 13degrees and even with the new cooling vests we got it still gets to be too much. So Arthur will be my gunner for now and I will drive for Casein have driven several times before but never during a mission with CPT Pike. Now with CPT Torres I have a chance to do what Caz has been doing this whole time and give him some time to relax on the FOB and call his family.

Caz has made his drivers hole a little comfortable for himself with pictures of his family hung up around him and a little cubby hole filled with snacks, books, and a sketch pad. He is a gifted artist and when we had down time on FOB Liberty I would ask him to draw up a few tattoos which I got from George.

As the day drew on it was getting hotter and hotter and we were racing up and down the main roads checking on all the platoons as they cleared. It was getting quite monotonous and I have no idea how Caz could spend an entire year up here without one complaint. It gave me a better idea of how much he had to tolerate with the heat, the constant driving without sleep, and all the gear he had to have on and still be comfortable up there. It really takes a special kind of person to put up with it and I know that not every driver could do it as well as Caz. Driving at night was a challenge all together because he had one small television screen behind the steering wheel that he could see where he was driving. The DVE (Drivers Vision Enhancer) was the camera/screen system that he used at night and it was easy to get tunnel vision. But luckily it was day time and I could drive with the periscopes.

I was starting to get a little jumpy at times having to try and spot for IEDs and several times I wondered how we made it through some of the roads without getting blown up. I wasn't as level headed as Caz and at one point found myself stripping off pieces of my uniform just to cool off a bit. The vest wasn't helping, I think it was leaking the cooling fluid making it harder to stay cool.

Towards the middle of the day we were heading down a main route and as I negotiated a couple of obstacles in my way I heard a loud bang from the engine compartment and a large ball of smoke came from the exhaust. The Stryker began to lose power and I knew we had blown the turbo. Blowing a turbo doesn't mean the vehicle wont drive but it loses a lot of power and the longer we kept moving the more we risk starting an engine fire.

We cross loaded CPT Torres to another Stryker and we decided to head back to the FOB for repairs. Getting any maintenance done on FOB Warhorse is a long drawn out process, since it's not our FOB we have to get parts shipped to us from other units or from FOB Liberty. I wasn't sure how long we would be here so we pulled up to the motor pool and began waiting for the Stryker to be fixed.

After a couple hours in the heat the mechanics told us that it wasn't in fact a blown turbo but the rubber boot that connects the turbo the power pack had come loose and would be an easy fix. They tightened the clamp on the boot and fixed the leak in the cooling vest and we were good to go. I jumped back in the drivers hole and reported to the Platoon that CPT Torres was with that we were on our way. As I pulled the Stryker out of the motor pool we heard the same loud pop from the engine compartment and once again the vehicle lost power. I yelled several swear words as I turned the Stryker around and pulled right back in to the same spot we were at before. Another hour or so passed and we finally made it back to CPT Torres and the rest of the Company to spend the rest of the day clearing the neighborhood. I really hope this is the last of our maintenance problems but usually in the hottest time of the year Strykers begin breaking down left and right so I am sure this isn't the last time.

25 June 2007, we finally moved further into the neighborhood and we had a tip that there were a few HBIEDs in the area so CPT Torres pulled our Stryker up close enough to scan the doors and windows with the RWS.I zoomed all the way on to the doorway to look for wires or trigger devices that might be detonated if dismounts entered. I noticed some wiring into the doorway so instead of risking sending anyone in we decided to try and detonate the house using a TOW missile. To give us a better chance we had a section of M1 Tanks attached to us and one of them pulled up next to my Stryker on the right and Georges ATGM on our left.

CPT Torres wanted me to mark the house with a few

rounds from my .5cal to show the ATGM and M1 exactly which house to fire at. I took aim at center mass of the house and fired off a 1round burst. They both saw where to fire and CPT Torres gave the okay for the tank to fire first. I have never been this close to an Abrahm firing so I stuck my head up out of the hatch. I pulled out my camera as the report came from the Abrahm, Round on the way was the signal that they were about to fire and a loud blast came from the large cannon that shook my Stryker and I yelled out, Hell yeah! as we saw the round enter the front of the house, out the back, through another building, across a road and through a large sign Holy crap! we all yelled out and CPT Torres started calling other units in the area to find out where the round went. It had stopped about 10meters away in another building. We all agreed that maybe they used the wrong type of round and a TOW would have better luck.

George and his crew took aim at the house and called up, On the way and the missile shot out of the Hammer Head of the ATGM. The missile hit the building, igniting the explosives already in the house and partially leveled the wall facing us. Part of the roof even fell in and we deemed the house all clear. Our next tip led us to another house adjacent to the building we had just fired at so once again I marked it with some rounds from my machine gun. The ATGM, once again, took aim and fired into the house making a smaller, yet effective, explosion inside the house. I was pretty excited to witness all this fire power and hopefully if any enemy were in the area it scared the crap out of them. Georges crew was pretty excited, I am sure, to be able to engage something again. There isn't much call for TOW missiles but since this area is so full of HBIEDs it's a lot safer than sending in our guys and risking losing them to a trap.

4 July 2007, still clearing Baqubah but today for our Independence Day we had our own celebration. We circled a large section of our Strykers into the make shift OP we set up in the housing area and got a chance to eat some hot chow and wait for night fall. We were given permission for another show of force which meant that we were going to fire as much crap off as we could. We had known enemy target buildings to drop mortars on and the Battalion Mortar Section was going to launch some Illumination Rounds over the city.

We sat around the housing area, I had my guitar and my buddy, Williams and I were playing and singing to try and take our minds off of where we were. We had our own version of the Bob Marley song, No Woman No Cry and I would sing the chorus as he would freestyle his own rap lyrics along with me on the guitar. It sort of reminded me of when I used to jam out with my boy, Evans.

A group of us were gathered around to listen and a group of local Iraqi Army guys were gathered around a fire making tea and joking with some of my buddies. These IA were different than we were used to and they seemed to be very passionate about us being in the area. They weren't shady like the IA back in our old AO and we actually got to have a little fun with them.

Night time finally came and to kick things off we had some extra Parachute Flares that I got to take in to the center of the OP and set off. We were so far away from home but we were able to make the most of the situation by having our own Fireworks show. Our Company Mortar guys were set up to fire on the Target Building which was an old Firehouse taken over by Anti-Iraqi Forces. As he started firing we watched and yelled as each round hit several hundred meters away right on the building creating large showers of sparks and flames. I had a pair of NVGs (Night Vision Goggles) which made the show even better.

Finally, the Battalion Mortars were ready to fire from their positions back on FOB Warhorse. Shot Over they called and we watched the sky around the city to watch for the first Illumination Round. A large POP and we could see the blinding light right above our heads, high in the air. As soon as the flair lit up we could hear a loud whistling sound, spinning over our heads. The large metal canister from the Illumination Round was falling towards us at a high rate of speed!

We dove under a nearby Stryker and started yelling to warn everyone to get under cover. The round crashed down on a nearby house that some of the IA were using to watch the light show. No one was hurt and our Forward Observer called the Battalion Mortar Section on the NET to warn them that the canisters were falling down on our positions. The canisters fire high up into the air and fire the Illumination Round with a parachute as it falls to the earth below, but if their calculations were correct the canister should be falling far away from us.

Another, POP and once again the canister fell down to the OP even closer to our Stryker They kept calling the Battalion Mortars kept saying they were adjusting but the canisters kept falling on top of us. Another round did the same and once again we dove for cover until finally the Illumination fire was called off completely. No one was hurt and we all laughed about it after it was over, but it was a little crazy to think that someone could have been hit by the heavy piece of metal. I remember, Smokey the Bear, used to come to my school as a kid, during 4th of July and would warn us of being safe with firecrackers, but this was a little bit bigger. The night settled down and we watched other Units around the city firing off hand-held flares and I decided to sleep on top of the Stryker that night, pretending like I was back home. I am sure that 4th of July will never be the same again and I don't think it will ever be this good.

17 July 2007, we are still pretty much homeless on FOB Warhorse. The unit here doesn't like us very much because they think we take up too much space. I think its bullcrap that we have to spend so much time in this area just to catch hell from them, while they get to chill out on the FOB. We get crap from them almost every time we go to the chow hall or the Internet Cafes we have to hole up in the tents that we were given which happens to be near the little airstrip where they launch the UAVs (Unmanned Aerial Vehicles) almost every half an hour. Every time I am about to close my eyes and sleep the little planes take off right over our tents and continue all night long. The Paladin Vehicles fire their large cannons throughout the night and we can never tell if its outgoing or incoming mortar rounds so we sit up in our cots every time they shake the FOB.

I guess we don't have it so bad here, at least we stay busy. The same rotations continue every day, one Platoon is out and we are resting. When it's time to switch we prepare the Strykers by heading to the ice point, filling the coolers with ice and bottled water and head back out for several more hours of clearing and area presence. Random little engagements erupt every once in a while but for the most part we have taken control of the city. I would think that the Units here would be glad to have us, since they couldn't do this themselves, but I'm not in charge so I don't have much control of it. That the life of a Stryker Unit; we are always needed but never wanted. Rumor has it that we are ending this crappy mission on the 15th of August so we will finally head back to FOB Liberty and be done with our tour. Almost there.

25 July 2007, a lucky break today literally. We are now moved into a different area of the city known as Old Baqubah and there are more people living in the area so we have begun doing more patrols than raids. We decided to hole up in a small alley for a couple days there and we got a call from another Platoon so CPT Torres wanted to go see what they wanted.

Caz backed the Stryker out of the alley and I began to spin the RWS around so it wouldn't point at friendly Strykers nearby and we made an abrupt stop; more abrupt than usual. Caz began winding up the engine and the Stryker wasn't moving. Well there goes the T-case. I said, not very happy. We had broken the Transfer Case which meant we couldn't move forward or backward.CPT Torres wasn't happy either and the only way to get it fixed was to get it back to the FOB. We called up a section of Strykers that were due for a break to hook up to us and pull us back to the motor pool.

CPT Torres decided to dismount and stay with a Platoon in the area and left Caz, Arthur and I on the Stryker. We slowly made our way back to the FOB which was a longer trip since we were being towed. There was no way to stop the transfer case from being further damaged on the way back so we had to put up with loud metal banging noises from inside the engine compartment and smoke began pouring in to the troop area. I quickly grabbed a fire extinguisher and began spraying through a hole to cool the transfer case and keeping the vehicle from catching fire. Arthur pulled security from the rear air guard hatch and about 3minutes later we were finally back in the motor pool.

The mechanics weren't happy to see what had happened because fixing the transfer case meant pulling the engine and taking apart some of the gunners area to get to the busted transfer case. It would take about four hours just to get it apart. Arthur and Caz decided to head back to the tent area to rest and get some hot chow while I stayed with them mechanics to help. They knew it wasn't our fault but the long trip back had caused so much damage that we would have to replace the entire engine as well.

Luckily, the engine we were getting had the ability to hook up an air conditioner which was now being added to the Strykers already in Iraq. A few of our Strykers already had them and we were pretty excited to get one. I didn't give a crap how long we were going to be in the motor pool we would be getting an air conditioner. It was like Christmas in July for CPT Torres when we called up and told him it would take all night and part of the morning but we would have AC!

Caz and Arthur came back to the motor pool to check on the progress and I was excited to tell them we were getting the new addition and they were equally overjoyed We got to work and helped tear apart the Stryker as much as we could but for the most part the mechanics had most of the job under control. Someone had to stay with the Stryker over night because we couldn't lock it up and, being the glutton for punishment I was, I told Caz and Arthur to head back and get some rest in the tent. I crawled up on top of the Stryker as soon as it got too dark to work and surprisingly the Sniper Netting made a nice little hammock.

I pulled out my iPod and looked up at the night sky. The sky in Iraq always seemed brighter, probably because it wasn't overpowered by city lights and smog. I laid there for a few hours just taking it all in and thinking about how nice it would be to fire up the Stryker in the morning and turn on the new air conditioner before we moved out.

Morning finally came and Caz woke me up from the top of the Stryker. I reeked of body odor by now, I hadn't had a shower in days and I quickly put on my boots to try and cover it up. The way of the grunt is to be able to get into the most dangerous areas for the longest amount of time, carrying the heaviest gear and getting the least amount of sleep.

Before we got Strykers this was how I was brought up and I still liked to embrace that mentality as much as I could even though we did a lot less walking. There were times where I didn't have to be on the Stryker and got to do a lot of dismounted patrols but now that I was a Vehicle Commander I spent most of my time holed up in the 2tons of metal, making it my home for most of the tour.

Other units that have different vehicles, like Bradleys or Humvees, like to call the Stryker a rolling RV but I didn't care because we knew we were different. I knew that the Stryker Brigade was the New Army and our way of fighting would begin to spread as it already has. Other Light Infantry Units are getting Strykers now and it's hard to go a day in Iraq without seeing a section of us rolling through the cities, kicking ass and taking names. We were the New Army.

Caz, Arthur and I got back to helping the mechanics and a few hours later we were done. The engine was back in and the new transfer case was ready to go. Caz jumped up in the hole and started it up to let the fluids circulate and I yelled up to the drivers area, fire up the Accad flipped a couple switches and the roar of the fans in front of me started up and immediately we felt cool air blow through the vents of the troop area It felt like heaven and I quickly called up CPT Torres to announce we were about to head back out into the city.

The air conditioner is different than a cars AC because ours is powered by hydraulic fluid so every time we heard an alarm go off in the vehicle we would have to shut it off to cool to fluids. As we made our way back to CPT Torres the alarm went off a couple times so we knew we had about a 1to 15 minute window of cold air, but for those few minutes we would enjoy it. Other Stryker VCs were pissed that we had the AC but we talked it off like it sucked and it wasn't worth the hassle.CPT Torres and the rest of our crew knew that we would have it a little easier here for the rest of the tour just knowing that we could have a little cold air every once in a while.

6 August 2007, no amount of cold air, down time, or hot chow could make this day ever go away. Another Company from our Battalion was clearing today and a squad went in to a house to clear it when the entire house exploded. Reports of the blast were all over the Battalion NET announcing that there had been casualties. Our jaws dropped when they announced that there had been four KIAs (Killed In Action) from the blast and one of them was a soldier that I had been pretty good friends with back on Fort Lewis. We were nearly finished with this crap hole and we had taken casualties. The Battalion was immediately called back in and the local units covered down on our areas.

We were all back on the FOB and the Battalion Commander, LTC Smiley, wanted to gather us all together by Companies to talk to us about the incident. Sadly we knew exactly what he was going to talk to us about because we had been through this before. It's never easy for a unit to lose any of their own soldiers, even if you don't know them. We all gathered around the BC as he talked us through the incident and he pulled out a dog tag chain full of tags that had the names of all the soldiers he had lost under his command. The chain was nearly full and it was a kick in the throat to see. My heart sank as he put them back in his pocket and wrapped up the talk by telling us that we would be part of a ceremony unlike I had never seen before.

That night the entire Battalion gathered in formation near a helicopter landing pad and we all stood at attention in line on either side of a walk-way leading to two Blackhawks still powered up. The Commander called us all to attention as our fallen brothers were carried down the walk-way to the helicopters for their Heroes Send Off. We all rendered a salute as they passed and I began to replay the last several months in my head. I remembered Dan and Kenney and all the others that had been taken from us this time. I remembered my friend, Jake Demand, who had been killed in our last deployment. I fought back tears of sadness and anger and as we dropped our salutes the bodies were put on the Blackhawks and they slowly lifted up in to the night sky.

The silence was deafening when the ceremony was finished. We walked slowly back to the tent and the unit there decided to give us a couple days off from missions to mourn the loss of our brothers. I don't think anyone slept that night but we all knew that we would have to eventually get back to work. There was nothing for us back at the tents, the phones were disconnected because of the whole thing so I put on my head phones and crawled in to my sleeping bag; morning couldn't come sooner.

CHAPTER 22
Last Ride to Liberty

15 August 2007, our last day in Baqubah, Caz, Arthur, Williams and I took the Stryker to the wash racks today to clean her up before heading back to FOB Liberty. We spent a couple hours just soaping and spraying it down. For the last several months this vehicle had been our shelter, our protection and our home so we wanted to drive her back in style. The Stryker was clean, full of fuel and ready to head back to Liberty.

I am not sure if what we did here made a difference but I do know that whatever problems any units had while they were in this city, we ended it. I looked around the tent as I packed up the last of my gear and finally it was time to line up the Company and begin the long convoy back to the FOB. Of course our last trip wasn't going to be easy; there was a large group of protestors blocking one of our routes back so we had to clear the route for ourselves and for the rest of the Battalion to move behind us.

We knew this was the only thing keeping us from finishing our tour so nobody in our Company really gave a crap what it took; we were going to get the job done. We began movement and not long down the route we began to see the group of protestors gathering to try and block us. As soon as we pulled up to the crowd, CPT Torres had Caz pull the nose of the Stryker towards a small group and knowing that the rest of the Battalion was behind us we had to move quick.

I was itching to fire of the last of my smoke grenades and CPT Torres gave me the go. 8 canisters popped from my grenade banks and a large cloud of white smoke spread across the crowd, quickly spreading them out away from the route. It didn't take long for other VCs to follow in the same footsteps and before I knew it the entire area was covered in white smoke. I scanned with my RWS as the smoke cleared and the crowd was pretty much gone. I guess they didn't want to play after all so CPT Torres called up to the Battalion Commander that the route was clear and we continued movement.

All the VCs were scanning carefully as we moved down the main route towards FOB Liberty and we weren't taking any chances. I was rocking music through the loud speaker as we sang along with excitement One long route separated us from completion and nothing was stopping this convoy, that's for damn sure!

Finally, the end was in sight as our lead Stryker pulled

through the gate. I stopped the music I was playing in the loud speaker and raised the barrel of my .5cal and began to pull the belt of ammo from the side. As we pulled past the guard tower I grabbed the microphone and screamed through the loudspeaker, Were back suckers did you miss us?!

We didn't even go to the motor pool, instead we pulled the Stryker as close to our living area as possible to begin downloading gear and equipment. Then, almost as soon as we began to drop the ramp someone announced over the Company Radio, Index! We were done Index was that sweet word we would hear at the end of a training mission to signal that we were complete We heard lots of shouting from all the other Strykers near us all we could see were hundreds of soldiers quickly pulling their gear off their vehicles. We knew we were done, but weren't taking any chances. We had to get the gun off the RWS so we couldn't be called up for patrols or bullcrap missions any more.

I looked back to a Platoon that had put up a large American Flag on the back of their Stryker in the celebration. No more patrols, no more long missions, no more heat or dirt, but best of all; no more losing buddies. The only thing that could get us now would be a lucky mortar round fired in to the FOB but there was no time to think about that crap now. We had to get all this equipment off the Stryker and in to our living areas before we could pack for the Freedom Bird to take us home. As Caz, Arthur, Williams and I were pulling off our crap from the Stryker we stopped for a moment to take one last picture together. We hugged each other and got back to work. As excited as we were, this was only the beginning of a long painful process of getting everything ready to go before heading back to the United States where the real party would begin!

1 September 2007, The last several days were filled with cleaning our gear, cleaning the Strykers, taking a break to get some Burger King, and back to cleaning the Strykers. We had to get them as clean as possible so they could be inspected before shipping them to port in Kuwait. Inspections were no joke; customs would literally look under the floor boards and seats looking for Iraqi soil or even weapons and drugs. It's sad to say that past units have tried and failed to sneak back war souvenirs and weapons in their vehicles and it only got them in trouble. I didn't think it would be a very good thing to spend 15 months in

hell only to get back and go straight to jail so we spent a lot of time making sure they were clean.

We were so close to being done that I could almost hear the sounds of the crowd that would be waiting to welcome us home. I remember coming back from our first deployment and we arrived at our Company, turned in our weapons and marched to the nearby gymnasium where all our family and friends were waiting to greet us. The marching band was playing and as we walked in I could hear the thunder of cheers. I wondered what it would be like for us this time. Would there be a large crowd? Would the band be playing as we marched in?

I think the most exciting thing I want this time is to meet Mindy face to face for the first time, but I don't know if she would be there since she was a little nervous to see my mom who would also be there with Wes and his wife. But for now we just relaxed as much as possible and cleaned our gear. We had to get all the dirt out of everything because we couldn't bring back Iraqi dirt in case it had germs and crap. Finally, after all this time we were going home.

CHAPTER 23
Welcome Home Tomahawks

13 September 2007, Gentleman, the Captain has now turned on the Fasten Seatbelt sign as we are beginning our final decent to McChord Air Force Base the flight attendant called on the intercom as my eyes began to slowly open from a very long nap. After several hours on a crowded plane I pulled my seat belt across my lap and looked around as all my buddies began to gather up the gear and stow their iPods and Laptops. I looked across the aisle to a window to try and get a peak as I felt the landing gear lower beneath us.

My heart began to beat with excitement as we broke through the thick Washington clouds and I could finally see something none of us had seen in a very long time; evergreen trees The engines began to wind down as we were getting closer and closer to touchdown and in a quick moment we felt the plane touch the runway. The screech of the wheels was deafened by cheers from everyone on the plane and the Captain came over the intercom for one final announcement, Gentlemen, on behalf of myself and the rest of our flight crew; welcome home! More cheers spread from the back of the plane and the we finally came to a stop.

As the doors opened we could feel the cool air sweep in to the cabin and in a moment we were all on our feet making our way, slowly, down the aisles. I finally rounded the corner and out the door to the steps leading to the tarmac below. I saw a camera crew at the bottom feeding live video back to the gymnasium full of families and I smiled as I passed by them. The first thing I noticed, aside from the beautiful rain clouds above me, was that it was freaking cold We had gone from 113 degree temperatures in Iraq to a steady 6degrees here and it was a welcome shock on my body.

We moved in a long file to the hanger where we were welcomed by Brass Officials and Commanders from near-by Fort Lewis. As we started settling in to the large building I made a quick call on a buddies cell phone to Mindy. I know my mom would be upset that I didn't call her first, but I really had to meet this girl who had captured my heart months ago. She didn't answer but I left her a message telling her that I was home and I would see her soon. I got everyone together and checked to make sure we had all our equipment and soon after began loading on to busses that would take us about ten minutes down the highway to our Company on Fort Lewis.

As we pulled near our Company Area I took in all the old familiar sights where we had used to work before leaving over a year ago. It was great to see that we still had all our old Barracks and Company building and we quickly downloaded the busses and moved into the Company area to turn in our weapons and equipment to the Arms Room. Celebrations continued and Mikeys wife had a few beers waiting for us after we were done. I cracked open a beer and sat down in our old office slowly taking my first sip of freedom.

Word came down that we had accountability of everything and we formed up to move to the gymnasium. The veterans from our first deployment knew exactly what to do and we quickly began marching. As we got closer to the gym we could hear cheers of people yelling and the Army Band was there playing to welcome us in. We paused at the doors to straighten ourselves up and as soon as we started walking in the band began playing the same song we got last time; Eye of the Tiger.

We slowly made our way into a large formation on the gym floor and I was careful not to tear up with excitement but it was hard to fight. I kept my composure and my head straight trying to spot Mindy or my friends out of the corner of my eyes and we finally came to a stop. The Brigade Commander yelled out at us, Battalion, Attention!

Silence swept through the large room as he gave us our welcome home speech but I didn't really pay much attention. After only a few minutes he yelled out those words that we had all been long waiting for; Gentlemen, Dismissed! In that sweet moment the floor was crowded with friends and families and I began to look around. I wanted to see Mindy before anyone else because I knew that once my mom got a hold of me she would try to keep me to herself. My mom was a little protective of me and she had been waiting for this for a long time, but I continued scanning for that beautiful red hair as if I was scanning a crowd for enemies.

I couldn't find her but as I pushed through crowds of soldiers and families giving as many hugs as possible I finally saw a familiar face. I looked up in to the bleachers and spotted a large handmade sign held up by my friends and my mom. I still hadn't found Mindy but made my way to them in hopes that they knew where she was. My mom moved in to the crowd and gave me a big hug, crying on my shoulder and as I returned the hug I looked up at my friends taking pictures of the whole thing. Wes and his wife, April, came to welcome me home and I was excited to see them all These were my closest friends from my home town in Missouri and after a few minutes of greetings I was ready to get out of the crowd.

My mom took my hand and began to guide me through the mess of people and I asked her if she knew where Mindy was. She told me that she was there and I began to get desperate. I didn't want to waste too much time because I didn't want to risk her leaving. I had to see her and as we moved through the crowd I somehow got separated from my mom and friends. I decided to take the brief moment to scan the crowd one more time with no luck. Where was she?

I began to move back out the doors of the gym to where we had left our bags thinking she might be there, but she wasn't was about to get upset as I turned around one last time and there she was, coming out of the gym. I don't know how I missed her but the only thing that mattered was that I found her and I couldn't help but think that I was staring at the most beautiful thing I had ever seen in my life. I walked up to her, nervous as a little boy. Here I was this big tough Army Soldier fresh from 15 months of kicking ass and I was nearly speechless. We gave each other a hug and she whispered in my ear, Welcome Home.

I told her that I had been looking for her and in a few, nervous words we agreed to meet up at Arthurs truck in the Barracks parking lot had to get all my bags up to my room before I could go anywhere and my mom, Wes and April helped me grab my gear to head about 5meters to the 3 story barracks before heading to the hotel where they were staying.

Once I had my gear in the room I told my mom that I would meet her in the parking lot in a few minutes but wanted to meet Mindy at my buddies truck. I could tell she wasn't too happy about it for some reason because I think she wanted to take me to the hotel but I had to see Mindy again. Before we had landed Mindy had helped my mom and friends set up a little welcome home party in the hotel and we were all supposed to go back and celebrate.

I finally got back down to the parking lot and met up with Mindy and Arthur with his family at his truck. Mindy was sitting in the back of the truck and wasn't saying a word. I made my way around to the side of the truck to see if I could make her smile. I don't remember saying much before leaning over the side and finally doing what I had been waiting to do for a long time. I kissed her for the first time, it wasn't the most romantic setting as she was holding a drink and we were being watched by all our friends around us but I didn't give a crap. It was a perfect kiss and I wouldn't regret it for a second because I wasn't going to mess this up. As I pulled away she looked right in to my eyes and smiled at me. With over a year in Iraq, getting shot at and getting hit by IEDs, taking many lives and losing very close friends, this was the perfect way to end it. With that kiss I finally knew I was home and I couldn't wait to get my new life started and hopefully find a way to forget everything that we went through over the last several months.

-END-

C co "Comanches" 1/23IN HQ PLT

SSG George Vash inside Baghdad Ink

SGT Apel (left), SPC Gary Doranski (right) shortly after getting blown up

SFC Toby Nunn, we ran into my old squad leader on our way home!

LTC Smiley, our Battalion Commander, with Tomahawk in hand giving a speech!

6436546R0

Made in the USA
Lexington, KY
20 August 2010